THE MAKING OF

My Fair Lady

*Al Hirshfeld's famous caricature used
for posters, programs, and cast albums.*

THE MAKING OF

My Fair Lady

KEITH GAREBIAN

ECW PRESS

CANADIAN CATALOGUING IN PUBLICATION DATA

Garebian, Keith, 1943–
The making of "My Fair Lady"

(Classic Broadway musicals)
Includes bibliographical references and index.

ISBN 1-55022-161-2

1. Loewe, Frederick, 1901–1988. My fair lady.
2. Lerner, Alan Jay, 1918–   . My fair lady.
1. Title. II. Series.

ML410.L63G37 1993 782.1'4 C92-095254-2

Illustrations are reproduced courtesy of the
New York Public Library for the Performing Arts.

Al Hirshfeld drawing reproduced by special
arrangement with Hirshfeld's exclusive representative,
The Margo Feiden Galleries Ltd., New York.
Cover and textual photos by Friedman-Abeles.

This book has been published with the assistance
of the Ministry of Culture, Recreation and Tourism
of the Province of Ontario, through funds provided by
the Ontario Publishing Centre, and with the assistance
of grants from the Department of Canadian Heritage,
The Canada Council, and the Ontario Arts Council.

Design and imaging by ECW Type & Art, Oakville, Ontario.
Printed by Imprimerie Gagné, Louiseville, Québec.

Distributed by General Distribution Services,
30 Lesmill Road, Toronto, Ontario M3B 2T6.
(416) 445-3333, (800) 387-0172 (Canada), FAX (416) 445-5967.

Distributed to the trade in the United States exclusively
by InBook, 140 Commerce Street, P.O. Box 120261,
East Haven, Connecticut, U.S.A. 06512.
Customer service: (800) 243-0138, FAX (800) 334-3892.

Published by ECW PRESS,
2120 Queen Street East, Suite 200,
Toronto, Ontario M4E 1E2.

TABLE OF CONTENTS

LIST OF ILLUSTRATIONS

For Judith
With Love

Introduction

THE COMMON LAMENT was "Broadway will never be the same!" when *My Fair Lady* finally ended its stellar run the night of Sunday, 30 September 1962. Millions of people had seen the show over six years and had helped break box-office records, even though Rex Harrison, Julie Andrews, Stanley Holloway, and Robert Coote did not stay with the cast throughout the six-year run. True, the Great White Way had been having an extremely lacklustre musical season in 1955–56 until *My Fair Lady* made its début, but this detail does not diminish the fact that the Lerner and Loewe show marked a glorious climax of a musical tradition. Besides affording civilized pleasure to millions, making an international star of Julie Andrews, and forging a new career for Rex Harrison, *My Fair Lady* used the substance and wit of George Bernard Shaw to add a new dimension to the Broadway libretto.

Had he lived to see the show, Shaw might very possibly have winced at the blossoming of love between Henry Higgins and his recreated flower girl, Eliza Doolittle, but Shaw would also surely have been charmed by some of the music and lyrics that helped make his own satirical points about language, class, and identity go down briskly and colourfully with audiences. *My Fair Lady* was a phenomenon that elevated musical theatre to a rare level of polished literate entertainment. It had a main plot of considerable substance, characters that had interesting literary and mythological antecedents, dialogue that was gilded literature, and music that was the very apogee of an operetta tradition. In short, the musical was — as Walter Kerr phrased it — "wise, witty, and winning."

But how did all the elements so conspire as to make this modern miracle? "Books about the Broadway musical usually provided the same old generalized information: who wrote it, who was in it, what it was about, and were there any hit songs." So remarks Steven Suskin, and so my book must depart from custom. Of course, any book on a musical must tell us what the show was about, but a better book must also describe *how* the show came about. It is very tempting for a writer to scrutinize yellowing, friable archives in order to re-visit a Broadway opening night, and recount just how deliriously excited the audience was when Julie Andrews, Rex Harrison, and Robert Coote broke into their ecstatic "The Rain in Spain" tango, or how the audience guffawed at Eliza's Ascot début, or just how impressed first-nighters were with the chandeliers that lit up the scene at the Embassy Ball. But such details are mere diversions — unless the writer explains the creative process that led up to the tango or the Ascot sensation or the radiant chandeliers. In short, a worthy book on a musical must go inside its material to inspect just how the show began, took shape, and had its final polish applied. Such a process calls, of course, for a combination of history, biography, literary criticism, and production data.

Any musical is a collaborative enterprise, where the past serves as prologue. In other words, a musical is not created *ex nihilo*. It has ancestors: parents and cousins, close relatives and distant kin. It may even have a very strange origin — as in the case of *My Fair Lady* which was based on a play by Shaw which, in turn, was based partially on a classical myth, partially on fairy tale, and partially on the playwright's personal experience. Before Lerner and Loewe there was Gabriel Pascal, and before Pascal was George Bernard Shaw, and before Shaw was Greek mythology and Cinderella. Before Lerner and Loewe, there was, too, an operetta tradition and an entire chronicle of Broadway composers and librettos. My book acknowledges these facts both in the history which it provides of Pascal and Shaw, and in the brief survey of the Broadway musical up to 1956 — the year of *My Fair Lady*.

Alan Jay Lerner was convinced that "the right people at the right moment in their lives embarked on the right venture — authors, directors, costumer, scenic designer, producer, lighting man, choreographer, and actors — and rather than extending their talents to the limit, expressed them to the limit." In other words, *My Fair Lady* was the sum of many parts, and my book is a story of how those parts were made to fit together.

There has never been a duplication of the success of this show. But how did Alan Jay Lerner dare to defy Shaw's anti-romanticism and get away with it? How did Fritz Loewe set a satire on a chauvinistic phoneticist to irresistible music? How did Moss Hart work ensemble magic with an Anglo-American cast? What were the technical achievements of the show? How did this work alter Broadway musical tradition? What was the legacy?

With these questions in mind, I have tried to take my readers on a journey of discoveries, using whatever means at my disposal — newspaper reports, videotapes, recordings, anecdotes, photographs, reference books — to show that such a journey culminated in a mid-century phenomenon of distinctive genuis.

Most of the leading figures from the original Broadway production are, alas, no more. They have gone into that good night called Forever. Disturbingly, no one thought it necessary or practical to film or tape the original production, and what little we have of the Moss Hart show survives in odd fragments — such as a black-and-white tape of Harrison's "rehearsal" of "I'm an Ordinary Man" with Franz Allers conducting, or a colour tape of Holloway performing "Get Me to the Church on Time" at a Tony Awards presentation, or an excerpt from an Ed Sullivan program of Julie Andrews singing "I Could Have Danced All Night." We do have the Broadway cast album and scores of photographs and slides, hundreds of clippings, and dozens of books either directly or tangentially related to the show. All these are ghostly remembrances of things past, but they do contribute to a synthesis of some value. They can help give some sense of how the show was put together. They are the trappings I have used for my journey of discoveries.

Shaw, Pascal, and Pygmalion

GEORGE BERNARD SHAW could hardly have forecast that his 1914 comedy *Pygmalion*, one of his "shameless potboilers" written, according to biographer Stanley Weintraub, "to oblige theatre managers or aspiring players," would have turned out to be a legend on stage, in film, and in musical theatre. Shaw himself called it "intensely and deliberately didactic," with a subject esteemed to be dry, and offered the fact of its public success as proof of his contention that "great art can never be anything [but didactic]."

The genesis of the play is only partly in the classical myth of a sculptor who, having made a beautiful ivory statue of a woman, falls in love with his own creation, despite an aversion to women whom he thinks of as prostitutes. In the myth, Pygmalion prays to Aphrodite to give the statue life, then marries Galatea and has a son by her called Paphus. Shaw's play also has a connection to W.S. Gilbert's *Pygmalion and Galatea* (1871), though Shaw's characters, dialogue, and plot are marked by his own distinctive wit and genius. Emotionally, the play derives from Shaw's attachment to Mrs. Pat Campbell, the actress of his passionate favour, the "Stella" of his most violent romantic yearnings. He wanted her to enact the leading female role and, so, become Galatea to his Pygmalion.

Integrating Faustian legend with Cinderella fairy-tale, and putting an emphasis on themes of linguistic and class distinctions, the play is about godlike powers of transformation. It is an Edwardian re-working of the Pygmalion myth, and converts the sculptor into a dry professor of phonetics who treats all women (except his own mother) with dismissive impatience, if not pure chauvinist scorn. When he comes upon a Cockney flower-girl with aspirations to a better life and social class, he pounces on the opportunity to put one of his pet theories to the test concerning the influence of economic circumstance on social and moral reformation. He wagers with Colonel Pickering, a fellow-linguist and author, that he can pull the girl, Eliza, out of the Covent Garden gutter and, by systematic tutoring, pass her off as a duchess.

Henry Higgins tries to be a little god or, at least, a scientific Pygmalion-Svengali. His Galatea or Trilby, however, refuses to fit into his preordained scheme of metamorphosis. Eliza Doolittle proves to be no mere marble statue, no doll, no enthralled pupil. Once transformed by her Prince Uncharming, she allows her own Life Force to carry her from the stage of a replica duchess at the Embassy Ball to the realm of an independent woman with a life all her own. So, Higgins who (like Faust) lusts after power, discovers that his experiment does not quite work out all to his own ends. Eliza rewrites all the legends that echo in the story: unlike Cinderella, she does not waltz off with her "prince"; unlike Galatea, she does not succumb to her "creator"; and unlike Trilby, she does not allow her own voice to be silenced by her Svengali.

Despite Eliza's independence, Shaw's play has a strangely paradoxical romantic undercurrent. Much of this derives from Eliza's own innate Life Force, a spark of feminine genius that is evident in the very first act of the play. Shaw very cleverly gives her subtle connections to the statuary Galatea — in the plinth on which she sits, sorting out her flowers, and in Higgins's reference to women as "blocks of wood." But she is no lifeless doll or statue who will submit to his mechanistic manipulation. Her wild cries and "boohooing" lack "the divine gift of articulate speech," but they are cries of the heart, and her street wisdom betokens a young woman who can survive in a tough half-world of Lisson Grove slum poverty, Covent Garden commerce, and Drury Lane seediness. Terrified of Higgins's note-taking, she proclaims her "respectable" character. Brushing off Freddy Eynsford-Hill's chivalrous solicitousness, she grandly hails a taxi, asserting a dignity that defies her wretched social circumstance. And when she shows up at Higgins's studio in Wimpole Street, offering to pay honest money for her speech lessons, she defies both his ridicule and mechanistic environment. Higgins himself is tremendously amused and impressed, though he characteristically misses signs of her individuality. Later, when she pulls off her coup of elegant deception at the Embassy Ball by seeming to be a princess, she transcends the dressmaker's art and Higgins's tutelage. She dares to speak in her own voice, and she severs her connection to him by walking out to a separate life with Freddy.

The original ending of the play has always been a problem for romantics and many realists. Although (in his specially written epilogue) Shaw adamantly insisted on Higgins's bachelordom and unamorous selfhood, and although his play makes it abundantly clear that Eliza is merely a social and scientific experiment that Higgins conducts with professional detachment, the ending does breed a certain ambiguity, reflecting (as Michael Holroyd puts it) "Shaw's uncertainties over his romance with Stella." For one thing, the ending is actually humanistic rather than mechanistic. It is human in its comedy of manners — Louis Kronenberger observes that "in England a comedy of accents is in itself a comedy of manners" — and in its characters, especially Alfred P. Doolittle, the uncommon dustman; Eliza, the Galatea who realizes what Pygmalion has not done for her; Mrs. Higgins, the worldly-wise, elegantly composed mother idealized by her son; and Higgins who, despite himself, is involved in a sexual subtext with Eliza. Inescapable, too, is Shaw's championing of Eliza's Life Force. When Eliza walks out at the end, her life is really beginning. In short, what started off purely as an experiment to Higgins becomes an experience to him. As Kronenberger notes, Higgins is too attached to his mother to have any capacity for romance. "Pygmalion isn't Pygmalion at all, he is Oedipus."

Audiences and performers have often sought to soften the ending and impose a romantic sentimentalism on a play that seeks to shun any middle-class agreeableness. The first London production in 1914 at His Majesty's Theatre boasted two great stars who were set on making certain modifications in the text. Mrs. Patrick Campbell did her own deliberate embroiderings on the role of Eliza, sometimes substituting deeply felt Freudian silences for Shaw's words. Commenting on this performance, Michael Holroyd notes that her exit line in Act 3, "Not bloody likely" — after her sensational "small talk" at Mrs. Higgins's At-Home day — nearly wrecked the play's balance when the actress perambulated the stage. And Beerbohm Tree, famous for his idiosyncratic innovations (such as a pet dog in *Richard II* and four miniature copycat Malvolios in *Twelfth Night*), wanted to take large doses of snuff, use a Scots accent, leap onto a piano from time to time, and indicate Higgins's addiction to port by walking with a limp and a cane. Ridiculed by Shaw for these ideas, Tree managed to emboss the production with other excesses. In one scene, he shoved his mother out of the way; in another, he appealed to Eliza to buy him ham for his lonely home, and sounded (complained Shaw) "like a bereaved Romeo."

On the opening night, Mrs. Campbell competed with Tree for outrageous effect. When her Higgins imperiously told her in Act 5 to stop off and buy him some Stilton cheese and a pair of gloves, she did a false exit in which she departed only to return a moment later and ask: "What size?" The audience roared and, according to Alan Jay Lerner, "the curtain fell, along with Shaw's jaw." But this was not all. Further sensation was to come, says Holroyd, in a piece of business in the brief interval between the end of the play and the fall of the curtain, when an amorous Higgins threw flowers at Eliza.

Holroyd points out that Shaw was bitterly upset by such theatrical liberties, but Tree claimed that audiences approved of such "improvements." Shaw wondered what had happened to English taste and instincts, and the public sense of proportion. He never yielded on the matter of the ending. He fumed at the "horrible gag" introduced in a Berlin production by a Higgins who suggested that he and Eliza shared the same bedroom, and he instructed Julio Brouta, his Spanish translator, that the actor who plays Higgins "should thoroughly understand that he is not Eliza's lover." After Eliza's departure, which Higgins should observe alone from a balcony, the actor should re-enter the room in excited triumph and exclaim, "Finished, and come to life! Bravo, Pygmalion!" Shaw hated the sentimental German and Dutch film versions of his play, though they were commercially successful, and he wanted no further movie treatments of his property. None, at least, until he met a swarthy

Transylvanian who was to become a version of Pygmalion to Shaw.

A Rumanian who, Lerner says, "claimed to be Hungarian and looked like a Himalayan," with his broad shoulders, high cheek-bones, strong head, dense black hair, and golden-brown tan, Gabriel Pascal had already achieved celebrity in Italy by directing films and selling them in Germany. *Populi Morituri*, in which he also played the lead, made him famous. He bought movie theatres and distributing companies, produced a film in England with Pola Negri, *The Street of the Lost Souls*, and later formed a partnership with the legendary Max Reinhardt in Germany for films for the UFA studios. These films — particularly the operetta *Fredericka* by Franz Lehar — were highly successful and established Pascal's name among the top German producers. Then, after a restless period in Hollywood, in which time he struggled to establish his credentials, Pascal decided that he would try to obtain rights to Shaw's plays because he admired this particular playwright above all others. Pascal professed the greatest admiration for *The Devil's Disciple* (indeed, a biography of Pascal appeared in 1970 entitled *The Disciple and his Devil*) because of its rogue-hero, and he himself came to be regarded as an entrepreneurial Dudgeon — eccentric, obsessive, and quite beyond conventional rules.

He had accidentally met Shaw in the early twenties at Cap d'Antibes on the French Riviera. While swimming in the nude on a blue-gold summer morning, he struck out for a red buoy that bounced invitingly far out in the water. Only when he was almost upon it did he notice someone attached to the buoy by a long, thin arm. Swimming closer, he saw a white head with a white beard and a skinny nude body. This turned out to be Shaw who, noticing the golden-brown of Pascal's buttocks and skin, asked his nationality and was told it was Hungarian.

Pascal revealed that he was fighting a rather hopeless fight in "the stinking *métier* of producing films." "If one day," Shaw said, "you are finally driven to the conclusion that you are utterly broke, and there is no doubt that you will be, come and call on me. Maybe then I will let you make one of my plays into a film."

In 1935, after an almost penniless voyage on a Dutch cargo boat, Pascal decided to approach Shaw formally. Rather "like Eliza Doolittle going to see Professor Higgins," he took a taxi to Shaw's cottage at Ayot St. Lawrence, though he well-knew that it was easier to obtain an audience with the King of England than one with Shaw. When he rang the doorbell, he was promptly met by a maid who informed him that Mr. Shaw was not seeing anybody.

"You go and tell your master," Pascal commanded, "that the film producer from Rome, whom he met in Cap d'Antibes about twelve years ago, is here. Tell him the young man with the brown buttocks."

"May I ask who sent you?" the maid inquired.

"Yes," Pascal replied, "fate sent me."

Shaw, on the stairs, heard this and hastened down.

"Who are you?" he asked.

"I am Gabriel Pascal. I am motion picture producer and wish to bring your works of genius to screen. Twelve years ago, you called after me from a red buoy that when I was utterly broke you would give me one of your plays. So we have a gentleman's agreement. . . ."

"Young man," Shaw cut in, "I am an Irishman and not a gentleman."

Pascal flashed a gypsy grin. "In India my guru told me that I am chosen by fate to make your works and message more widely known through films. So here I am. Your man. . . . I think we could start with *The Devil's Disciple*. Since my boyhood I have wanted to direct and play *The Devil's Disciple*. I am Richard Dudgeon."

For the first time in his life, Shaw found himself virtually speechless. "*The Devil's Disciple*, indeed."

"Or . . . we could start with . . . *Pygmalion*."

"Is that all you want? And may I ask you, young man, how much money do you have?"

Pascal pulled out a few coins that remained in his pocket after the taxi ride to Ayot. "Twelve shillings," he declared.

"Come in," said Shaw. "You're the first honest film producer I've ever met."

Shaw quickly came to see that Pascal was what Holroyd calls "an extraordinarily clever and dramatic talker" who could concoct the most fantastical scenarios of his own life history, portraying himself in these fictive memoirs as a series of almost mythic heroes — an orphan and a gypsy, a daring circus acrobat, a street urchin, a rebel military cadet in Holics, a prodigy in the Viennese theatre world, a descendant of Metternich or, perhaps, Talleyrand, an aristocrat of mysterious parentage, an ex- Hussar, a penniless pilgrim in India, and a movie tycoon. Shaw was greatly entertained by these flashes of self-dramatization. Really, the man belonged in one of his plays. Pascal was oblivious of money and seemed to have the soul of a Dubedat or Dudgeon. In Pascal's biography Shaw's personal secretary, Blanche Patch, related that "GBS never met a man who entertained him more." Quite unperturbed by Pascal's grammatical deficiencies, Shaw "had found another spellbinder like himself, and a man whose soul was not for sale." Yet Shaw did not actually rush into giving him film rights. Shaw lacked confidence in movie studios, primarily because they thought of texts as commodities that could be mercilessly and carelessly altered in exchange for generous sums of money. Numerous movie greats had wooed Shaw for movie rights — from Harry Warner and Alexander Korda to Louis B. Mayer and Samuel Goldwyn. When Shaw had eventually agreed to films of *How He Lied To Her Husband* and *Arms and the Man*, the results had been disastrous. But Pascal seemed like a man who knew his job and Shaw's plays, and Shaw finally granted him rights to several of his great plays — including *Pygmalion, Arms and the Man, Major Barbara, Caesar and Cleopatra, The Devil's Disciple, The Doctor's Dilemma*, and *Saint Joan*.

Pascal was especially charmed by *Pygmalion* but discovered that bringing it to the screen was no fairy-tale. He was told that Shaw's name was box-office poison ever since the dismal flop of his two filmed plays. He was told that Shaw was too highbrow for the movie public and that the plays were too literary for screen treatment. According to Pascal's wife and biographer, Valerie, "*Pygmalion* was the deadliest play of all since it did not have enough action for a two-reel short, and worse, it did not have a happy ending. As a matter of fact, it had no ending at all: it left the audience and Eliza Doolittle in the air." So no studio would touch the play. Pascal's rival, Alexander Korda, did want to do Shaw, but not with Gabriel, and Pascal was too proud to ask for a loan. When another prospective financier wanted improvements on the play through the addition of plenty of sex, Pascal calmly spat cherry pits in his face and walked out of their meeting. Not long after this, the miracle did happen, and financial backing was received by Pascal Films.

Shaw made certain that he remained in touch with the production by adding scenes and giving numerous detailed suggestions. Among the many new scenes added were ones of Eliza's first bath at Wimpole Street, Freddy's lovesick loitering outside Higgins's home, a sequence between Freddy and Eliza on the street, and a later Covent Garden scene when Eliza realizes that she cannot go home again. "I must have two policemen," Shaw argued with Pascal on 16 April 1938, "one aged forty and the other aged twenty, and two scenes, because I must produce the impression of the two lovers having run at least as far as Cavendish Square from the first policeman." In the matter of the leads, Shaw approved of Wendy Hiller as Eliza, but felt that Leslie Howard was too much of a matinée idol to be a good Higgins. Shaw felt that Howard's elegance would endear him to the public and that audiences would probably want him to marry Eliza, which is just what Shaw did not want, having argued in his Epilogue to the play that "Galatea never does quite like Pygmalion: his relation to her is too godlike to be altogether agreeable." But Howard had box-office appeal and was also listed as co-director. Later Shaw approved of Jean Cadell as Mrs. Pearce and asked for Violet Vanbrugh as the Ambassadress at the Embassy Ball — a scene, by the way, he agreed to expand. He also suggested making the Queen Rumanian, with an attendant black princess speaking Hottentot (all clicks), followed eagerly by Higgins who would frantically record all the clicks in his notebook. But Pascal was too Hungarian to allow these changes, and Shaw accommodated him on the insistence that the Queen and Crown Prince be Transylvanian and that Eliza be suspected of *Hungarian* royal blood. Shaw also obliged Pascal by renaming Higgins's bombastic pupil Karpathy and by having this character say of Eliza, "Only the Magyar race can produce that air of divine right, those resolute eyes."

The black-and-white film, co-directed by Anthony Asquith and Leslie Howard, and with camera work by Jack Hildyard, boasted a brilliant cast, sets by Laurence Irving (of the great theatrical family), costumes by Worth and Schiaparelli, music by Arthur Honegger, and script additions by W.P. Lipscomb and Cecil Lewis. Its camera-work and montage effects now seem dated and strange, with quick dissolves and fades, and close-ups that favour Higgins too early in the story. The opening is more Pascal Studio than Shaw, with a close-up of flowers followed by a medium close-up of Eliza, a tracking shot of the market-place, a dissolve to evening, the rumble and crack of thunder, tolling bells, Cockney lowlifers, a close-up of Higgins eavesdropping on them, then the downpour of rain in Covent Garden.

Leslie Howard, whom Shaw felt would be too romantic for his role, sounds dry and almost ascetic as he adjusts Eliza's straw boater while insulting her. Back in his laboratory, he wears glasses, and in one shot he makes a silent but imposing voyeuristic god. Wendy Hiller's Eliza is heartfelt from the first moment, although she can possibly be faulted for making the character too snivelling with tearful regret after the comic climax at Mrs. Higgins's At-Home tea-party — a scene, by the way, for which the film invents two characters, a parson and his spouse, to complete a very English comedy of manners. There are interesting bits of acting in the minor parts, especially by Jean Cadell who uses a Scots accent for Mrs. Pearce, David Tree as a boyishly eager and tickled-pink Freddy, and Esmé Percy who is a handsome Karpathy, but the most outstanding portrayal is Wilfrid Lawson's as a sturdy, husky-voiced, grimy and sleazy Doolittle, authentically from the gutter, gap-toothed and with a rasp to make one's hair stand on end as he makes the most improper suggestions with amoral bluffness.

Visually, the film seems quite modest by present standards. Mrs. Higgins's At-Home party is much plainer than expected, with extensive lace for the matriarch, and very ordinary garb for the others. Even the Embassy Ball scene is tastefully Edwardian rather than extravagantly eye-catching. Eliza appears in a backless satin gown with a long train, long gloves, a double strand of pearls, and a coronet, but her costume stands out by its simplicity.

The film's great achievement is its literateness, just as its most startling innovation is the un-Shavian ending, where the highly dramatic conflict between Higgins and Eliza is worked out contrary to Shaw's design. Heavy script editing and romantic acting by Howard shift the register of Higgins in particular, and though he is superficially the proud, devilish chauvinist, Howard gives him an achingly soft vulnerability and a slower delivery to add weight to his words. When Eliza proclaims defiantly, "I can do without you. Don't think I can't," he retorts with sensitivity, "You never asked, I suppose, whether I could do without you?" Then when Eliza tells him that he will have to do without her, his old pride flares up, before modulating to a new-found remorse: "But I shall miss you, Eliza. I confess that humbly and gratefully. I've become accustomed to your voice and appearance. I even *like* them rather." Eliza retorts: "Well, you have them both on your gramophone and in your book of photographs. When you feel lonely, you can turn the machine on." The classic conflict between mechanism and humanism is emphasized in this line, and Eliza tries for the clincher: "You've got no feelings to hurt." "I can't turn your soul on," Higgins complains. Eliza is furious at this devilish machination, recognizing his ability to "twist the heart in a girl as some can twist her arms to hurt her." She wants a little kindness, but Higgins is insensitive to that. He is more perturbed by the fact that his "masterpiece" appears to be heading for a wasteful life with Freddy. And for a brief while it appears that all is lost for Henry Higgins, when Eliza drives off with Freddy. In the final sequence, Higgins walks out into the street and wanders alone and disconsolate. Upon his return to Wimpole Street, he smashes things in frustrated rage and then turns on the machine with Eliza's recorded voice. Unexpectedly, he suddenly hears Eliza's real voice overlapping the recorded one. The Shavian ending is reversed, and Higgins resumes his former imperiousness, though now somewhat muted, as he asks: "Where the devil are my slippers, Eliza?"

The film ending is a breach of the logic Shaw elaborately constructed in his Epilogue. Aware that Shaw would never permit such a romantic liberty with the text, Pascal conspired with Lipscomb and Lewis to keep secret this significant alteration. At the sneak preview, Pascal held tightly to Charlotte Shaw's hand while her husband's white beard glowed fluorescently in the dark. When the movie concluded, Shaw was wordless, but smiled faintly. His wife, however, turned to Pascal and remarked: "This is the finest presentation of my husband's work." The film earned an Oscar for Shaw's screenplay and the Volpi Cup at the 1938 Venice Film Festival. It went on to break box-office records and make Wendy Hiller an international celebrity, and Shaw a star to be mentioned around Hollywood along with the name of Garbo.

Putting aside his disapproval of the ending, Shaw proudly wrote to Pascal: "An all-British film, made by British methods without interference by American script writers, no spurious dialogue, but every word by its author, a revolution in the presentation of drama in the film. In short, English *über alles*." Accordingly, he considered Pascal a godsend. Charlotte Shaw, according to Holroyd, recognized that Pascal's enterprise and vitality had done wonders for her husband's spirit, actually making the playwright feel twenty-five years younger. "I am Cagliostro to Shaw," Pascal boasted. "I keep him alive fifteen years more." "Pascal is doing for the films what Diaghileff did for the Russian Ballet," Shaw later wrote in a foreword to Valerie Pascal's memoir of her former husband. "Until he descended on me out of the clouds, I found nobody who wanted to do anything with my plays but mutilate them, murder them, give their cadavers to the nearest scrivener without a notion of how to tell the simplest story in dramatic action and instructed that there must be a new picture every ten seconds and that the duration of the whole feature must be forty-five minutes at the extreme outside." Shaw loved the fact that Pascal was hypercritical of the script writers who infested his studio in an attempt to tinker with the playwright's original work. "[He] thought that everything they did was wrong and that everything I did was right. Naturally I agreed with him." Shaw expressed his gratitude by deeming his friend "a genius."

This genius had, in a sense, become a Pygmalion himself to Shaw by taking control of the playwright's literary property, by presenting the master in a new medium, and by elevating the modern film to a polished literate level. A foreigner with hardly any sophistications of English grammar, he was the newly acknowledged proprietor and propagandist for a prose stylist of the first rank. And so thoroughly was Pascal committed to Shaw's plays that when in a 1943 interview he remarked that he would never get married, Bernard Shaw's retort was, "That's right. He is wed to my plays."

The Idea of a Musical

PASCAL WENT ON TO FILM *Major Barbara* in 1941, starring Wendy Hiller (one of his film discoveries) in the title role, Robert Morley as Andrew Undershaft, and Rex Harrison as Cusins. Next he did a lavish production of *Caesar and Cleopatra* in 1945, with Claude Rains, Vivien Leigh, and Flora Robson. But neither was a box-office or critical success to match *Pygmalion*, and though his wife and biographer says that he and Shaw discussed possibilities for American productions — *Arms and the Man* with the Lunts or Ginger Rogers, *Candida* with Katharine Cornell, *The Millionairess* with Marlene Dietrich, and *The Devil's Disciple* with a number of stars, including Clark Gable and Cary Grant — none of these ideas materialized.

Perhaps, then, it was logical for Pascal to exploit his success with *Pygmalion*, even if this meant distorting the form and texture into a musical version. But precisely why he wanted to musicalize this play remains a point of speculation, especially as he knew of Shaw's refusal to grant permission for any musical adaptation. Holyroyd recounts how for years after the Pascal film, Shaw "made the same reply to all composers and resisted every pressure to 'degrade' his play into a musical. 'I absolutely forbid any such outrage,' he wrote in his ninety- second year. *Pygmalion* was good enough 'with its own verbal music.' " And yet Gabriel Pascal, one of his staunchest disciples wanted to go expressly against the master's voice and grain.

Was Pascal now too much a Pygmalion himself to resist testing his own manipulative power? In *The Disciple and His Devil*, her touching memoir of her former husband, Valerie Pascal builds up a strong impression of his dominant personality and erect will. She describes his mixture of arrogance, tenderness, and cruelty, and refers to his youthful attempts to find himself in characters such as

Peer Gynt, Faust, Til Eulenspiegel, and Byron's Manfred. She sketches his spell-binding personality and his interest in the idea of metamorphosis and self-recreation, and she alludes to his repeated manipulations of people and careers. In his private life, Pascal commanded the turbulent romantic passions of several women, having multiple affairs simultaneously, and in his public life he was even more influential. It was Pascal who sought to promote and then end his wife's acting career; it was he who discovered and magnified the filmic talents of Wendy Hiller and Deborah Kerr; it was he who tried to extend the fame of Jean Simmons; and it was he who had made Shaw a household name in Hollywood.

In the early spring of 1952, while in Tinseltown to produce *Androcles and the Lion* with Jean Simmons, Victor Mature, and Alan Hale, Pascal phoned Alan Jay Lerner who was also in town to do the screen play for the musical, *Brigadoon*, the hit Broadway show that Lerner and Frederick Loewe had created five years earlier. Lerner knew who Pascal was, but did not quite realize how forceful and eccentric the producer could be. Pascal invited — ordered — him to lunch at a popular restaurant called Lucy's, and there Pascal sat like a Buddha, ordering four plates of spaghetti (one for his guest and three for himself) and four raw eggs which he cracked over the pasta.

"I want to make musical of *Pygmalion*," he declared in a voice that had "the timbre of a 78 record played at 33," recalls Lerner. "I want you to write music."

Lerner hastened to explain that he didn't write music.

"Who writes music?"

"The composer. Fritz Loewe."

"Good," Pascal said. "We will meet again and you will bring man who writes music."

This matter settled by decree, Pascal launched on a discourse about Shaw's sex life, which he claimed was non-existent, before moving on to Gandhi's.

After lunch, he performed his major dramatic gesture by urinating in public while awaiting the arrival of his car. As on-lookers gaped, he tucked himself in, zipped up, got into his car, and drove off.

Lerner was never able to be embarrassed again.

Alan Jay Lerner was born in New York City on 31 August 1918, and was educated at The Choate School and Harvard. The middle of three sons, he was his father's favourite and pampered by frequent visits to Broadway musicals. By the age of twelve, he had only one ambition "and that was to be involved, someday, somehow, in the musical theatre." He had studied piano from the age of five and had begun writing songs in his early teens. His mother had studied singing "in that semi-serious way dowagers' nieces did at the turn of the century." (Her accompanist was Richard Rodgers's mother.) She contributed to his knowledge of concert halls, museums, and ancient ruins by many European trips, while his father — a chauvinist with a passion for boxing — instilled in him a deep affection for the English language and for all things English.

Lerner claimed in his autobiography to have become a professional librettist "because of a cigarette on a golf course, a left hook to the side of the head and a wrong turn on the way to the men's room." His memoir clarifies this cryptic epigram by detailing how he was expelled from The Choate School in Connecticut after he was caught smoking on the golf course, and how as a result of this, he was "punished" by his father by having to spend four years at an American rather than European university. At Harvard, he contributed to the Hasty Pudding shows, the annual undergraduate musical romp, saw the Boston try-out of every play and musical *en route* to Broadway, took flying lessons, and went out for the boxing team. Which is where the left hook on the side of the head came in and permanently damaged the retina of his left eye.

With his one good eye he deserted the familiar places and faces of his youth and frequented the Lambs Club (now extinct), where he met Lorenz (Larry) Hart, the first man who ever encouraged him to believe that he might have a future as a lyric writer. From the Lambs he moved to the Hotel Royalton, also on Forty-fourth Street, whose most famous resident at the time was the critic, George Jean Nathan, who lived "in a room without ventilation and so thick with [cigarette] smoke" that the bellboy who delivered morning coffee "could never find him." After a year and a half here, Lerner moved across the street to the illustrious theatrical hotel, The Algonquin. During this period he was writing five daytime radio shows a week and the lyrics for the Lambs Gambols. In late August of 1942, while having lunch at the grill, Lerner found near his table "a short, well-built, tightly-strung man with a large head and hands and immensely dark circles under his eyes." The man had lost his way to the men's room. Lerner recognized him as Frederick Loewe, a Viennese-born ex-concert pianist and a talented but struggling composer. Loewe was the son of Edmund Loewe, a celebrated singing actor who played the role of Prince Danilo in the Berlin production of *The Merry Widow*. After his parents immigrated to America in 1923 and his father had suddenly died, Frederick became a cowboy, a professional boxer, a beer-garden pianist, a pit-pianist, and the composer for *Great Lady* in 1937. Now through the capricious wind of chance, Lerner and Loewe had met each other, thus beginning a collaboration that eventually involved them in Pascal's dream.

In the early forties, Lerner and Loewe wrote two unmemorable musicals — *Life of the Party* (1942), which ran nine weeks, and *What's Up?* (1943) about an eastern potentate whose plane is forced to land at a girls' school. The second musical was called "ill-advised" by Lerner and "awful" by Loewe, and it was said (by Gene Lees, their biographer) to have "died of its own deficiencies." Their next work, *The Day Before Spring* (1945), was, according to Stanley Green, "a highly literate and imaginative fantasy which just missed being a hit." The partners' luck changed radically with *Brigadoon* (1947), which established them in the front ranks of the American Musical Theatre. Though it was far from faultless, containing some songs that were too heavily and pretentiously solemn for a light romantic piece, it had a freshness of setting, and its story of faith and love moving a sleepy old town to miracles, compensated for some of the shortcomings. Robert Lewis directed with sensitivity, Oliver Smith designed evocative settings, and Agnes de Mille made each dance sequence — most notably the Sword Dance, the Chase, and the Funeral Dance — an integral part of the story. Moreover, two songs, "The Heather on the Hill" and "Almost Like Being in Love" were instant commercial hits. Their next musical, *Paint Your Wagon* (1951), was a rollicking Gold Rush story that had force and zest despite a tendency to ramble. Lerner and Loewe had allowed their extensive research into miners' dialogue and history to swamp the fun, and Walter Kerr complained that the librettist seemed to be "more interested in the authenticity of his background than in the joy of his audience." There were outstanding numbers in it — such as "Wand'rin Star," "They Call the Wind Maria," and "I Talk To the Trees" — but the show was only a modest success by Broadway standards, and Lerner and Loewe failed to become Broadway legends. Until Gabriel Pascal and his idea for *Pygmalion* as a musical.

Both men were aware that the property had been offered earlier to a number of eminent composers, such as Howard Dietz and Arthur Schwartz, Cole Porter, E.Y. Harburg and Fred Saidy, and Rodgers and Hammerstein, all of whom declined the invitation, according to biographer Gene Lees, because of what they thought were insoluble problems with the project. Rodgers and Hammerstein both realized that the drawing-room ambience of *Pygmalion* and the text's deliberate non-romanticism were drawbacks to a musical form. Yet both Lerner and Loewe knew instinctively that *Pygmalion* was an ideal challenge: the strong period setting and the conflicts between Higgins and Eliza were perfect material for Loewe's musical composition style, because, as Lerner says, he could "musically characterize a period or a locale, providing it [was] not contemporary, without losing his individuality and, at the same time, make it contemporary"; and the Shavian verbal score — witty, precise, pointed, given to arias and duets — provoked Lerner's sensitivity to language and to English style.

Early into their work on the play, however, both men were on the verge of admitting defeat. No matter how hard they tried, they "did not seem to be able to tear down the walls of the drawing room and allow the play to unfold in a setting and atmosphere that suggested music." The play seemed incapable of obeying certain rules for the construction of a musical. An ensemble was necessary, of course, but where would it come from? The men thought of setting the play at Oxford, where Henry Higgins would be a professor of phonetics. Then the ensemble would be undergraduates. However, Lerner felt that this was not only "obvious," but "clumsily uninspired and useless." A proper musical at the time demanded a sub-plot for musical variety. *Pygmalion*, however, had only one story — superb though it was — and characters or story-line could not be invented without grave costs to Shavian integrity. Most of all, the play was "a non-love story," and how could the team write "non-love songs"?

A chance meeting with Oscar Hammerstein at a Democratic Presidential rally at Madison Square Gardens simply consolidated Lerner's doubts. Hammerstein shook his head hopelessly, telling Lerner "It can't be done. Dick and I worked on it for over a year and gave it up." A few weeks later, Lerner and Loewe abandoned the project, and so *Pygmalion* remained unmusicalized until the summer of 1954, when Gabriel Pascal died.

Several dramatic things had happened to Lerner and Loewe in the period before Pascal's death, but the most significant one was the separation of the two as business partners. Feeling "an ever-widening separation" between himself and his period, Lerner had separated from his partner, who began a new musical with Harold Rome. Lerner's fortunes declined along with his health: he developed brain fever (encephalitis) which led to spinal meningitis, delirium, and a paralyzed left leg. When he recovered enough to resume work, he attempted to musicalize Al Capp's popular hayseed cartoon, *L'il Abner*, and approached Burton Lane to do the music, and Herman Levin (with *Call Me Mister* and *Gentlemen Prefer Blondes* as credits) to serve as producer. Matters, however, did not proceed smoothly. Lerner realized that he was "munching on 'alien corn'." Capp became increasingly restless, and Levin suddenly disappeared on a Mediterranean cruise at the invitation of film producer, Sam Spiegel.

Lerner found himself drifting back to the idea of *Pygmalion* as a musical. He lunched with Loewe and immediately felt as if he were "going home." For the first time in two years "the thin line of a distant dawn on the horizon" appeared, and he felt "like a long-distance runner slowly catching up with the herd."

The collaborators discovered to their amazement that, as Lerner later recalled, "many of the self-same reasons that made the project seem impossible two years earlier were now in its favour." The "rules" of musicals had changed. Realism had started to toughen up

American musicals, and the accent on emotional reality (already seen vividly in Kurt Weill and Brecht) cancelled the traditional need for a sub-plot or a singing chorus as an integral personality to characterize locale. Lerner and Loewe discovered that their adaptation did not require the addition of any new characters to impart more variety. They decided to follow the screenplay more than the stage version, and to add business that occurs between the acts. For example, the interim between Higgins's departure from Covent Garden and Eliza's arrival at Wimpole Street the next morning was filled (in the film) by a short sequence in Eliza's dwelling. A little later, there was another scene between Eliza and her dustman-father in order to establish his character through a song ("With a Little Bit o' Luck"), leading right into Eliza's appearance at Higgins's home.

As to the general technique for the music and lyrics, it was decided that the outstanding aspects of the main characters should be those dramatized — hence Eliza's wistfulness in "Wouldn't It Be Lov-erly?", Higgins's passion for language in "Why Can't the English?", and Freddy's romantic yearning in "On the Street Where You Live." Most of all, words and music had to reveal what was *implied* rather than already stated in the text. There had also to be moments when Shaw's drama would be assisted when it did not by itself reach certain peaks.

One of the most dramatic episodes about the musical occurred behind the scenes, so to speak, and involved the acquisition of rights owned by the Pascal estate which was then under attack by two women — one, his former wife, Valerie, and the other, The Woman of Shanghai, a dragon-lady who claimed to be Pascal's fiancée. Further, whichever party won the rights from the Pascal estate would have to face another obstacle — the Shaw estate in London. Besides, Lerner and Loewe were not the only ones in quest of the rights to *Pygmalion*. The Chase Bank (later the Chase Manhattan Bank) had been named the executor of the Pascal will, and Metro-Goldwyn-Mayer, who intended to acquire the rights for themselves, had poured much money into this bank, so the studio had a favoured position. Loewe, however, was not discouraged. "My boy," he said to Lerner, "there's only one thing to do. We will write the show without the rights, and when the time comes for them to decide who is to get them, we will be so far ahead of everyone else they will be forced to give them to us."

When Herman Levin returned from Europe and called Lerner to see how he was getting on, Lerner answered, "Very well."

"Have you found a way to do it?" Levin asked.

"I think so."

"How does Lane like it?" Levin inquired.

"I haven't the slightest idea."

"Why not?"

"Because he's not doing it, Fritz is."

It soon became startlingly clear that Lerner was no longer speaking about the *L'il Abner* project, but of *Pygmalion*. And there was no time to lose.

Accordingly, the production team set about selecting designers and cast. The simplest decision was in the choice of scenic designer. Tall, courtly Oliver Smith was immediately chosen for his rare ability to achieve mood, perspective, and beauty in his painting for the stage. Smith had fled to New York from Penn State when a wealthy relative promised him a course at the Yale Drama School, provided Smith could make his own living for a year. The eager lad served as an usher at Roxy, a stock clerk at Stern's, and a bookstamper at the Flatbush library. Seduced by the charms of New York, and flourishing on $20 a week, he put aside his Yale dream, and got his first designing commission to do Massine's *Saratoga* for the Ballet Russe de Monte Carlo in 1942. This led to a commission for Agnes de Mille's *Rodeo* the same year, and two years after that he was doing his first work for the American Ballet Theatre, creating sets for *Fancy Free*, the Jerome Robbins-Leonard Bernstein ballet that later became *On the Town*. In a very short time, Lucia Chase invited him to become a co-director with herself and Agnes de Mille. Designing for ballet proved to be of very great importance to his eventual work in the theatre, because it taught him the economy of space, while provoking his powers of fantasy and poetic sense. Ballet design sharpened his painterly eye, and Smith specialized in romantic realism. His successes with musicals such as *Rosalinda* (1942), *Billion Dollar Baby*

(1945), *Brigadoon* (1947), *High Button Shoes* (1947), **Gentlemen Prefer Blondes** (1949), *Guys and Dolls* (1950), *Paint Your Wagon* (1951), *La Traviata* at the Met, and a revival of *Pal Joey* (1952) challenged the received vocabularies and ideas of critics. Able to be sculptural, architectural, and painterly at the same time, Smith insisted that a design should not be an egotistical statement. He wanted it to be modest, yet truthful. But *My Fair Lady* would compel him to have a design that was far from modest.

The ideal man to do the costumes was Cecil Beaton, of whom Lerner said that it was difficult to know "whether he designed the Edwardian era or the Edwardian era designed him." He was at his creative peak in this period, able to draw upon his vast knowledge of history and detail, photography, and high fashion. His skill at photography had enabled him to meet and photograph many great celebrities, from Garbo, Izak Dinesen, and the Sitwells to Diaghilev, Oliver Messel, Margot Fonteyn, and Vivien Leigh. The camera afforded him artistic control of situations because he was able to pose and arrange people, and to use the technology as a go-between. His early photographic career, according to Boze Hadleigh, was spent "shooting" society matrons who "wanted immortality *before* they became pendulous." Accordingly, he gained celebrity by creating a portrait gallery of the famous, but more than being his passport to social fame, photography was a valuable prelude to his theatre designing because it helped his eye find special and attractive details with which to gild his soul and senses.

Normally, Beaton preferred designing both sets and costumes, but having the reputable Oliver Smith as a close partner calmed his hyper-sensitive ego. Oliver Smith later noted that their artistic partnership was a great test of friendship and mutual respect: "We were both internationally acclaimed scenic stars, both extremely ambitious and aggressive. . . . Once the tug of war was over, he was friendly and collaborative."

There was no doubt in Lerner's mind that the most interesting and complex character in *Pygmalion* was Henry Higgins whom he believed to be a projection of Shaw in his articulateness, intellectual ardour, and wittily concealed loneliness. And Rex Harrison was among the first actors considered for the part — though, contrary to Lerner's "white lie" in his memoir, Harrison was not the very first star approached by the producers. In his 1967 book *Wiv a Little Bit o' Luck*, Stanley Holloway, who was to play Alfred P. Doolittle, claims that Noel Coward was given top consideration, followed by Michael Redgrave, George Sanders, and even Sir John Gielgud. Coward's biographer Sheridan Morley says that it was Coward himself who suggested Harrison to the producers.

Lerner had met Harrison and Lilli Palmer (his wife at the time) when Harrison was appearing as Henry VIII on Broadway in Maxwell Anderson's *Anne of the Thousand Days*, a role for which he was to win the 1949 Tony Award as Best Actor. Indeed, Harrison and Palmer were frequent house-guests of Lerner, but when Kurt Weill proposed a new English version of *The Threepenny Opera* for the English actor, Lerner was startled. "Does he sing?" he asked incredulously.

Weill replied, "Enough."

This remark stuck in Lerner's mind and he reported it to Loewe and Levin.

In 1954 Harrison and Palmer were starring in *Bell, Book and Candle* in London's West End. Another Coward biographer, Charles Castle, relates that at that time, Harrison was once again lending proof to Coward's claim that next to him, Rex was "the finest light comedy actor in the world." When Lerner and Loewe telephoned him to ask if they could visit him and discuss their project, they sensed by his answer that he thought that they had, as Lerner put it, "gone around the bend." But his curiosity was aroused just enough to agree to a meeting early the next January.

Two months before this meeting, the newspapers caught scent of the project, and Lerner received a phone call from Mary Martin's husband, Richard Halliday. Martin was still starring in *Peter Pan* on Broadway, and as two of her fans, Lerner and Loewe were delightfully surprised by her apparent interest in their new work. But the idea of Mary Martin as Eliza Doolittle was, to say the least, a little unusual. However, as "one never knows the limits of a great star's talent," and as Lerner remembered Lorenz Hart's advice not to say no to a star for at least twenty-four hours, he and Loewe decided that there was nothing to lose to share with her their early songs from the show. They had composed "The Ascot Gavotte" for the famous tea party (which had been shifted from Mrs. Higgins's home to the race track), "Just You Wait 'enry Higgins," "Please Don't Marry Me" (a first attempt to dramatize Higgins's misogyny), "Lady Liza" (Higgins's song to reassure Eliza before the Embassy Ball), and "Say a Prayer for Me Tonight" (about Eliza's misgivings). When they played these five songs for Halliday one afternoon, he was "*most* enthusiastic." They agreed to his request to repeat the performance for Mary one night after *Peter Pan*.

Neither Lerner nor Loewe was living in New York City at the time, so the meeting was scheduled for the apartment of Lerner's mother a few nights later. Shortly before midnight, Martin, Halliday, and their guest, Mainbocher (the famous couturier), arrived and listened in silence to the five songs and departed almost immediately after the final song. "Only Main made any comment — saying he liked them very much," recounts Lerner. Not having heard from Martin or Halliday for a week, Lerner called Halliday whose tone was serious and almost secretive. Halliday asked for a luncheon meeting two days later at the Hampshire House, where he announced gravely in his heavily accented Southern voice, "Alan, you don't know what a *sad* night that was for Mary and me. Mary walked the floor half the night, saying over and over again, '*How* could it have happened? How *could* it have happened? Richard, those dear boys have *lost their talent*.' " Too stunned to respond, Lerner waited for the next blow. "Alan," Halliday continued, " 'Just You Wait' is simply *stolen* from 'I Hate Men' in *Kiss Me, Kate*, and the 'Ascot Gavotte' is *simply* not funny. It's *just* not *funny* at all." Halliday had nothing to say about the other three songs, but his verdict was so benumbing that Lerner changed the subject quickly, gulped down his lunch in three mouthfuls, and left. The last words he remembered hearing were: "I'm *so* sorry. *Really*, Alan. We're *so sorry*."

Upon hearing his partner's account of this episode, Loewe retorted with classic understatement, "Well, I guess, they didn't like it."

Stanley Holloway recounts that with Mary Martin definitely out of the running as Eliza, the two men considered Deanna Durbin and

Dolores Gray, but discarding these names, they set out to investigate the new young star on Broadway in *The Boy Friend*, Sandy Wilson's genial satire on what theatre scholar Gerald Bordman calls "the gay, unpretentious confections of the jazz age, carefully and accurately burlesquing the simplistic plot lines, the formula songs (the Charleston number, the dream of a love nest, the exchange of vows, etc.), and the stylized staging of the period." Both show and ingénue lead were British imports and appealed to Lerner's Anglophilism. Julie Andrews was a mere nineteen years of age, but had received rapturous praise for her dazzling gifts: a charming, crystal clear soprano voice, immaculate diction, dancing grace, physical attractiveness, and stylish acting. Lerner was moved to write: "From the moment she set foot on the stage, one could see she fairly radiated with some indefinable substance that is the difference between talent and star. Whatever that substance is you know it is there because you find yourself caring about him or her spontaneously and illogically, far beyond the dialogue, the role, or the play. The substance is not always the same. Gertrude Lawrence, for instance, was electric; Laurette Taylor was all humanity; Julie was all that is endearing."

Born Julia Elizabeth Wells in Walton-on-Thames, Surrey, eighteen minutes south of London, the teenage sensation had been sent at eight to a singing teacher who confirmed that the girl had "an enormous, belting, freak voice with a range of five octaves and some fierce high notes," according to biographer Richard Windeler. "I sounded like an immature Yma Sumac," Andrews once remarked self-deprecatingly, though she also realized that she was "one of those child-brat prodigies" with "an immensely powerful voice" for her tender age. "It was to everyone's great surprise that it was there; there were no real vocal musicians in my family." But show business had, indeed, made an indelible impression on her mother and stepfather, for Barbara Wells had been a pianist for a variety show at a seaside music-hall at Bognor Regis, where she met guitarist Ted Andrews, who had emigrated from Canada as a vaudeville entertainer. Julie's first big break came with a single aria, "I Am Titania," from *Mignon* which she sang for a revue, *Starlight Roof*, at the Hippodrome. She was only twelve at the time, but reached F above high

C with ease, and captured all the critics' notices. The year-long Hippodrome run led to an invitation to appear at a Royal Command Variety Performance at the Palladium on 1 November 1948, headlined by Danny Kaye. When she repeated the aria, she became the youngest soloist ever to perform for royalty at the Palladium. Next, she toured music halls across Britain, played in Christmas pantomimes — such as *Aladdin*, *Cinderella*, and *Humpty Dumpty* — before getting trapped in a disastrous musical, *Mountain Fire*, where she was a young Southern woman (with an awful accent) made pregnant by a travelling salesman. Fortunately, *The Boy Friend* was her next credit. She played Polly and found herself in a home-grown West End hit. American producers Cy Feuer and Ernie Martin wanted to retain the flavour of the English original, so they imported the entire show to Broadway, where Julie Andrews became the new toast of the town.

Opening night at the Royale Theatre found most critics enthralled with the show in general and with Julie Andrews in particular. Brooks Atkinson of the *New York Times* deemed the show "a delightful burlesque," called Dilys Lay's Dulcie "a miniature Beatrice Lillie," and then added: "It is probably Julie Andrews, as the heroine, who gives *The Boy Friend* its special quality. She burlesques the insipidity of the part. She keeps the romance very sad. Her hesitating gestures and her wistful shy mannerisms are very comic." The show became a box-office success, and Andrews won above-the-title billing.

She spent a year in the production and remarked that the experience was one of the best in her life. "I learned a lot about timing and comedy from American audiences. I used to be a slow learner, and it was a marvellous experience to learn on the job and get away with it."

In April, 1955, slightly past the mid-point of her year in the show, she was called by a representative of Lerner and Loewe who asked when she would be available for a new musical. At eighteen she was the exact age for Eliza — though none of the actresses who had ever played the role before was even close to eighteen. At her audition, she read a couple of scenes for Lerner and Loewe, and a few days later, she and Lerner worked in a studio on a mixture of scenes from other plays. Her ease and composure impressed Lerner, and when she showed what he called an occasional "flash of fire and, at one point, a sudden downpour of tears," Lerner was delighted by the feeling submerged in her Walton-on-Thames middle-class pleasantness. He reported to Loewe and Levin that "quite possibly there was a lot more to Julie Andrews than met the eye and ear." Lerner and Loewe urged her not to make any other commitments until they had acquired the Pascal rights. She shot back, "Lovely," and they parted.

By the end of November, the Chase Bank decided to ask the court for permission to appoint the most celebrated literary agent of the time, Harold Freedman, to make the all-important decision of Pascal estate rights. Upon hearing this, Lerner and Loewe quickly rushed in to ask Freedman to be their agent, and a few days later, he notified the court that he had decided in favour of awarding the rights to Lerner and Loewe. By also notifying the court of his role as the men's agent, he established his honesty and trustworthy judgement.

By selling his share of family stocks in a gold mine to the tune of $150,000, Lerner was able to bankroll his next significant enterprise — the producing team's expedition to London to snag Harrison and a few others and to gain more information for the musical. Lerner had not returned to England since 1937 — not even for the opening of *Brigadoon* in 1949 or for *Paint Your Wagon* three years later — but as he drove with Loewe from Heathrow, London began to come alive for him again.

At a backstage meeting with Harrison, the trio found what Lerner remembered as "an unmistakable strain and *froideur* in the air" — not just in his dressing room but in his wife's as well. They later discovered that the two stars were unofficially separated off-stage and that Harrison was in love with the brilliant comedienne, Kay Kendall, whom he joined every night after he and Lilli Palmer had completed their curtain calls. Because of the secrecy of this affair and the strain of maintaining a certain respectable façade with Palmer, Harrison was under great strain, a fact exacerbated by the intensive and vulgar scrutiny of journalists who sniffed around for scandal. Harrison was a difficult man to get to know at the best of times, and at this sensitive time in his life, he was not easy to persuade to attempt a musical version of Higgins. He hated the two songs already composed for the role, and said so promptly. Lerner and

Loewe knew instinctively that he was right, with Lerner commenting in his memoir: "The songs were slick and instead of being acting pieces set to music, they were skin deep and clever word games." It took considerable effort to reassure him that these versions were, by no means, final products. Next, they had to convince him that Leslie Howard was not the definitive Higgins of our time. When they ran the Pascal-Asquith film, Lerner crystallized his entire argument against Howard's interpretation by pointing to a single line in the scene after the ball when Higgins is taking full credit for Eliza's triumph. At the point when the two characters are alone, Eliza cries out, "What is to become of me?" and Higgins responds, "Oh! That's what is worrying you, is it?" To Lerner, Howard's delivery indicated a full awareness of Eliza's pain and of "the strange stirrings within himself." Lerner thought this quite wrong, for Higgins is not supposed to have the slightest idea of what is troubling her and he is meant to be genuinely amazed by the discovery. Lerner recalled how Harrison finally agreed with him that Leslie Howard was "a touch too romantic."

The next question was whether the actor could do a musical at all. Lerner and Loewe invited him to try a song in their room at Claridge's, and when he tried a verse of "Molly Malone" to piano accompaniment, Loewe stopped him: "Fine. That's all you need." Lerner noted a "tenor timbre, which meant it would carry over an orchestra and, we later discovered, his sense of rhythm was faultless." Harrison, in short, was "instinctively musical," but his dithering left the pair hanging around London for weeks and using their time to visit Covent Garden and learn how Cockney rhyming slang works — which was especially useful for Eliza's number, "Wouldn't It Be Loverly?" with its clever dialect touches. The Cockney habit of inserting words into the middle of other words inspired the use of "absobloomin'lutely" in the lyric. As they wandered around the market, they saw a group of costermongers warming themselves around a smudgepot fire. This image was to be reproduced in the musical.

A couple of days after their Covent Garden visit, the two began work on Eliza's first song, with Lerner realizing that "it had to be about the longing for creature comforts." He gave his partner the title "Wouldn't It Be Loverly?" and Loewe wrote the melody in one afternoon, creating a cheerfulness characteristic of the Cockney spirit.

The pair had time to meet with Cecil Beaton and then with Stanley Holloway who loved the idea of playing Alfred P. Doolittle. Holloway had begun his career as a boy-soprano in English music-hall and converting to baritone in 1921 when he began a six-year run as soloist in the hugely popular satire "The Co-Optimists." The show was a prototype of all those bright, witty revues for which London became famous, and it became something of a national institution with what Holloway calls its method of "digging at pomposity, ridiculing the ridiculous and laughing at the ludicrous." And all this was done "with good humor and without bitterness, bile, or belligerence." Holloway moved on to a stretch of comic monologues, impersonating Albert Ramsbottom and his cantankerous family and, best of all, Sam Small (a brainchild of the performer), who was the epitome of all Lancashiremen. Described by his creator as "a North Country lad," who was "sometimes perky, sometimes dour, but always independent; a tough son of a gun who knows his point of view and his rights and isn't afraid to speak up for them," he was a naïve, gentle, and lovable character who got into various predicaments. It was natural for Holloway to move into musical comedy (*Hit the Deck, Song of the Sea*), the legitimate stage, and then film, but what was significant was the range of his acting experience on screen — from Vincent Crummles in *Nicholas Nickleby*, a bit part in Pascal's *Caesar and Cleopatra*, and a small role in David Lean's classic *Brief Encounter*, to a memorable Gravedigger in Olivier's *Hamlet*, rich, roguish Lockit in Peter Brook's *The Beggar's Opera*, and Alec Guinness's partner-in-crime in *The Lavender Hill Mob*. A favourite with working-class Englishmen as much as with the country's royal family, Holloway seemed quintessentially Old England "roast beef," solid and hearty but not to be taken for granted.

In 1954 Holloway was playing at the New York Met in *A Midsummer Night's Dream*, the Old Vic production that had originally opened at the Edinburgh Festival. This was the show that generated a great quip from one of his close friends: "Fancy Stanley going in for Shakespeare. The man's gone from top to Bottom!" It was in October of that year that Holloway had first heard vague rumours of the impending musical version of *Pygmalion* from someone named Paul England. The rumour was confirmed by Lerner and Loewe — but only after a long delay.

Many months later, over lunch at Claridge's, they asked him if his singing voice was still intact after his long absence from the musical stage. Lerner recalls that without a word "he put down his knife and fork, threw back his head and unleashed a strong baritone note that resounded through the dining room, drowned out the string quartet and sent a few dozen people off to the osteopath to have their necks untwisted." (Holloway's account differed from Lerner's by being more sedate and not so richly comic or operatic.)

As soon as his contract was settled, Holloway went to Berman's, where he had been a customer for nearly forty years. He was determined to have authentically British clothes for the show because he felt that "when you are playing a British rôle — and especially a character rôle — only British-made clothes seem . . . to look remotely authentic." The store made the dustman's outfit mainly out of stock, "except for a specially made dustman's shovel hat." And for Doolittle's wedding scene, Berman's made him a smart set of tails and top-hat, "just slightly over-ostentatious, as Doolittle obviously would have chosen." The boots were "good, solid policeman's boots with a heavier sole clumped on."

Lerner remembers that on the Sunday of the fifth week, Harrison called and suggested that they all go for a walk in Hyde Park. The trio must have seemed ridiculously incongruous to onlookers, for the actor was over six feet tall while the Americans were only slightly over five feet each. Moreover, Harrison used long, brisk strides, whereas Lerner and Loewe had to jog along to keep up with him. This lasted for almost three hours, Harrison "chatting away," Lerner and Loewe "panting away." Then all at once he stopped, turned to them, and said: "All right. I'll do it." Lerner and Loewe were too exhausted to register any joy. Before they parted, Harrison remarked to Lerner: "I don't know why, but I have faith in you."

Bell, Book and Candle was expected to close by late spring, so Lerner and Loewe notified Holloway and Beaton that rehearsals would begin in New York in early autumn. They advised Harrison to take some vocal lessons — not to learn how to sing, but to exercise his cords and tempi. According to Harrison in his 1991 memoirs *A Damned Serious Business*, he then went daily to a male teacher of *bel canto* in Wigmore Street in London who attempted in vain to convert the actor into an Italian who could roar with his voice. Lerner then referred the actor to Bill Low, a pit-conductor at the London Coliseum, who gave him a rough idea of how to steal a music-hall trick of talking on pitch. Harrison tried it on "I'm An Ordinary Man," and it worked beautifully, making a difficult technique seem almost effortless. Harrison's great sense of rhythm helped him remain true on the note. "If you talk flat or talk sharp it's just as bad as singing flat or singing sharp. You've got to sing right bang in the middle of the note, you've got to talk in the middle of the note," he wrote with authority many years later.

In mid-February, recounts Lerner, he and Loewe left London with "the Shaw rights in one hand, commitments from Rex Harrison, Stanley Holloway, and Cecil Beaton in the other, two less songs than [they] had arrived with and a year's work ahead of [them]."

Back in New York, they retired to Rockland County for the long haul, but before settling down to more work on the book and lyrics, they addressed themselves to the problem of financing the play. They contacted Robert Sarnoff, the president of NBC, and their mutual friend, Goddard Lieberson, the vice- president of Columbia Records, a division of CBS. Lieberson was influential with William Paley, president of CBS, but no financial deal was forthcoming for awhile, so Lerner and Loewe got down to the business of finding a director instead. Herman Levin had suggested Moss Hart, most celebrated for his collaborations with George S. Kaufman on *Once in a Lifetime* (1930), *Merrily We Roll Along* (1934), *You Can't Take It with You* (1936), a Pulitzer Prize winner, and *The Man Who Came to Dinner* (1939). Hart had authored on his own such plays as *Lady in the Dark* (1941), *Winged Victory* (1943), and *Christopher Blake* (1946), and had written books for musicals with scores by Rodgers and Hart, Cole Porter, Irving Berlin,

Kurt Weill, and Ira Gershwin. So, he obviously understood lyric writing. In 1946 he wrote the screenplay for the Oscar-winning *Gentleman's Agreement*. In addition to these brilliant credits, he enjoyed the reputation of being a superb constructionist who could analyze the most subtle weaknesses in a script.

But Hart was writing a musical himself at the time with none other than Harold Rome — the very person Loewe had once partnered during his earlier professional separation from Lerner. It was decided to wait until a few more numbers had been composed before presenting the directorial project to anyone.

Lerner and Loewe were determined to retain as much of Shaw's dialogue as possible, which automatically meant that their musical would have more dialogue than any other musical to date. As Lerner put it, "The only way to accomplish this, we felt, was to fill the score with tempo and to search every emotion until we found that aspect of it that demanded it." A case in point was "Show Me," which was preceded by a long scene and which appeared after Eliza leaves Higgins's house, not knowing where she can turn. Normally, her sad mood would have led to a slow, sad song, but "an emotion is a mountain with many sides," so Lerner and Loewe translated her hurt and fury into passion and that passion into tempo. "Fritz decided on almost a Spanish tempo and wrote it in an agitated 5/4."

Loewe was a master of improvisation, spending hours at his task while Lerner sat and listened, occasionally jotting down an idea for a lyric. Surprisingly, Lerner developed a bad case of writer's block, which lingered for four weeks during which time he lost eight pounds. In desperation, he consulted a psychiatrist who remarked, "You know, you write as if your life depends on every line." This was certainly a valid observation, but no more so than Lerner's own realization of the profound impact of the Mary Martin-Richard Halliday incident which had shaken his self-confidence. Once he admitted this to himself, he cured his own paralyzing fear. Ever after, when either he or Loewe was stuck, one of them would say to the other, "You *poor dear* boy. You have *lost your talent*," and so burst the blockading tension with cathartic laughter.

After "Wouldn't It Be Loverly?" was fully composed, the duo

turned their attention to the part of Henry Higgins. Because of his strong acting personality and vocal style, Rex Harrison quickly became interchangeable with Higgins in Lerner's mind. The composer learned that the secret in writing for the actor was "to make certain at all times that the lyrical and musical line coincided exactly with the way one would speak the line. For example, 'Let a woman in your life and your sabbatical is through' was composed in such a manner that it could either be spoken or sung without altering the music." Harrison's mode of *sprechstimme* or spoken-song was derived not from the German tradition but from the English music-hall which had patter songs (as in Gilbert and Sullivan, Noel Coward, or Stanley Holloway), in which words were spoken to the rhythm of a tune. As Harrison once wrote of this, "It's an old and evocative form, and you get much more meaning into words when you use the music as underscoring than singers can do when they sing them. This is because you can give full weight and true expression to them. With ordinary singing, especially opera singing, you're thinking much more of the noise you're making. You can't give words and music equal weight, you see, that's the trouble."

Lerner and Loewe began to realize that Harrison's songs, many of which are comic, had to be built on a strong foundation of emotion. So, "Why Can't The English?" which began as a mere statement of an intellectual position, became underscored by anger and frustration. "I'm an Ordinary Man" (which replaced "Please Don't Marry Me") was informed by amiability intersecting with violently hysterical misogyny. "A Hymn to Him" softened this mixture into a satirized sense of frustration. And Higgins's most romantic "I've Grown Accustomed to Her Face," which grew into a standard hit, finally released the character's long-suppressed and hitherto undisclosed yearning and loneliness.

While engaged in some of these concoctions, Lerner and Loewe finally heard of CBS's agreement to finance the entire production, budgeted at $400,000, and of an offer by Columbia Records to produce the cast album. The next accomplishment was the signing of Moss Hart as director.

Hart gave his enthusiastic approval to "I'm an Ordinary Man" and

"Why Can't the English?", so Lerner and Loewe returned to Harrison, beaming with new confidence. Harrison added his approval, but his show, *Bell, Book and Candle*, was doing so well at the box-office that no rehearsals of the musical could be scheduled as yet. Without a firm rehearsal date, the entire production could conceivably fold. However, after some artful negotiations with *Bell, Book and Candle*'s English producer, Hugh "Binkie" Beaumont — and through the mediation of Irene Selznick — an agreement was reached about a November closing for Harrison's play in return for a cash settlement and rights to the English production of the musical, which as yet had no official title.

With January 3 set as the first day of rehearsal in New York, Lerner and Loewe continued "a parlor game" with titles. *Liza* and *Lady Liza* were rejected, according to Lerner, "because it would have seemed peculiar for the marquée to read: 'Rex Harrison in *Liza*'." *Come to the Ball* was considered, as well as *My Fair Lady* for a short while, but Loewe preferred *Fanfaroon* — a rarely used English word meaning someone who blows his own fanfare — because it rhymed loosely with *Brigadoon*. The parlour game remained inconclusive.

A return visit to London to try out two songs on Harrison bore mixed results. The actor loved "I'm an Ordinary Man" on first hearing because it was (in his words) "a brilliant, long and complicated number, but with a very easy soft-shoe rhythm, with a lilt to it and an easy delivery." "Why Can't the English?", however, worried him because "it sounded far too much like Noel Coward, too reminiscent of 'Mad Dogs and Englishmen'; it needed breaking down and changing, it had a too familiar tang."

As work continued on revisions and the rest of the score, the other technical departments were also receiving concentrated attention. Lerner remembers that Moss Hart wanted Abe Feder to light the show, and all agreed, even Cecil Beaton who was aware of Feder's reputation of lighting actors first and scenery second. But Feder had worked magic with lamps, with border, spot, and footlights, with projections and extensions of the spectrum applied to fabric and décor. He had created the lighting for *I'd Rather Be Right* (1937), Orson Welles's *Doctor Faustus* (1937), *Hold on to Your Hats* (1940), *The Boy*

Friend (1954), and some twenty productions of the American Ballet Theatre. Moreover, he had conceived the lighting plot for the New Coliseum at Columbus Circle, and had solved the difficult problem of lighting President John F. Kennedy's last birthday party, held in two ballrooms on either side of the foyer of the Waldorf-Astoria. Beaton joined Hart for conferences on the costume design, and gave palpable evidence of a mania for the right colour, texture, and material. His reputation, of course, preceded him, for Lerner had been forewarned by "Binkie" Beaumont of Beaton's absolute dedication to his craft. For Noel Coward's *Quadrille* (1952), starring Alfred Lunt and Lynn Fontanne, he sent his assistant all across London and then to India in search of rare silks and luxurious fabrics. When she returned after two months of assembling an extravagant collection, Beaton examined the swatches wordlessly and when he had finished, he looked up and said: "Lily Taylor, you're just not trying."

Beaton was thoroughly a product of the Edwardian age, an era that he described in his 1989 book *The Glass of Fashion* as "a period of gaiety, when life was so inexpensive that a dandy with four hundred pounds a year could go out dancing most nights of the week, wearing lavender gloves and a wired button-hole in the lapel of his tail coat." Beaton's fastidious eye for fashion apparently developed early in his crib, for he recalled the women's hourglass shapes, pouter-pigeon bosoms, protruding posteriors, and hats that were "enormous galleons of grey velvet with vast grey plumes of ostrich feathers sweeping upwards and outwards." His "inward child's eye" always "sought out the detail rather than the conception as a whole. A particular trimming on a dress could make a profound impression" on him.

Many of these early memories were revived in his theatre designs, and his great talent was a confirmation of the Edwardian urge to be distinctly different. This urge was personified by three women of his youth. One was his mother, who dressed in "miraculously soft materials" and who loved to bear "a large special bunch of imitation lilies of the valley on her bosom, pinned to a pale green chiffon scarf." His Aunt Jessie, who married a Bolivian, was more flamboyant and enjoyed fashion. Several times a year she would make trips to Paris and return with enormous black trunks filled with dresses, shoes, corsets, ribbons, ruffs, aigrettes done up in black tissue paper, yards of velvet, brocade, lamé, and "chiffons gaily iridescent with sequins." Her hat-boxes held six hats apiece — "vast discs covered with funereal plumes of black ostrich feathers or white ospreys; hats for the evening and hats for the afternoon; hats for her garden parties."

The third, most important influence on young Beaton was his first theatrical heroine, Lily Elsie, who "at that time was the queen of London's musical comedy, the English creator of *The Merry Widow*, and perhaps the first actress of her genre to captivate the popular imagination by means of her ladylike restraint and dignified grace." This gentle creature with a swan-like profile exuded a sweet sadness, and Beaton obtained a picture of her in a black hat, a short brim at the front, a large one at the back, adorned with wisps of paradise — a "Merry Widow" hat that created a craze for huge hats.

There were numerous other influences on Beaton, from the theatre world, the candlelit *demi-monde*, and the aristocracy — but the "first creature of artificial glamour" he ever knew about was Gaby Deslys, "something of an actress and something of a dancer," who was "a key transitional figure — the successor to the grand Parisian *cocottes* of the nineties on the one hand," and as a theatrical figure, "the precursor of a whole school of glamour that was to be exemplified twenty years later by the Marlene Dietrich of the Cinema screen." Beaton loved her artifice and her near-vulgar self-adornment with jewels, plumage, and furs that gave the word "bizarre" new overtones. Her signature was luxury — a quality that Beaton dearly loved to use in his theatre designs, especially for *Lady Windermere's Fan*, *The School for Scandal*, and *Quadrille*.

Fortunately for the Shavian musical, he was able to find the materials he needed right in Manhattan, though after Abe Feder had demonstrated how the lights would bleach out many of the costumes, Beaton had to resume his search for fabrics. He selected extraordinary pastel shades for the ballroom scene, and for the Ascot Gavotte he re-created the stunning black, white, and grey palette once seen at Ascot the first season after the death of popular King

Edward VII. At this time it was customary to dress period musicals in the styles of the 1900s. Beaton wanted to use the fashions of 1914 — those of the time when Shaw originally wrote the play — but he met with opposition. "Surely they won't be sexy" was the protest. He promised they would be. "You're sure it won't look like a comic strip?" Moss Hart worried. Then, too, perhaps the women would look too much like vultures. Beaton decided that the "magpie" effect was the solution. This pleased Moss Hart, so the other chiefs simply shrugged and gave their assent, according to Beaton's biographer Richard Buckle. Beaton evidently looked upon the musical as an opportunity to put on stage all the memories stored up since his early boyhood: "Never had any theatre assignment given me so much pleasure," he remembers in his 1964 book *Cecil Beaton's 'Fair Lady'*. "Suddenly, a myriad childhood's impressions were paying dividends: haphazard pieces of the jig-saw puzzle of memory suddenly started sorting themselves into place." Remembered, for example, was Elfie Perry's dinner frock of striped silk; that would be "perfect for Eliza's last appearance." The enormous Madame Triana's garden party dress of grey and apricot was also an inspiration, along with his Bolivian Aunt Jessie's enormous cartwheel hats, and his own mother's Malmaison, "with circular pink cardboard back-reinforcement," grey satin, and ostrich feathers.

Before Beaton and Oliver Smith completed their designs, Hanya Holm was signed on as choreographer. She was settled upon after Gower Champion had insisted on terms that could not be afforded, and after Michael Kidd had incensed Moss Hart by his rude reaction to Lerner and Loewe's music. The producers were aware that their show did not require a great deal of dancing, but they wanted the choreography to be an integrated thing rather than a showpiece for virtuosos and production numbers. Born Johanna Eckert in Worms, a few kilometres from Mainz on the Rhine, she had married a painter-sculptor, Reinhold Martin Kuntze, and then had met Mary Wigman, the great dance teacher who struggled against audiences' conservative tastes. Johanna Kuntze, disliking the heaviness of her names, renamed herself Hanya Holm to create a clever match of etymology and alliteration, according to her biographer Walter

Sorell. She regarded Wigman as the Eleanora Duse of the dance. Wigman and her company performed frequently in Germany, Italy, and other countries, and Holm remained with Wigman as chief instructor of the school in Dresden. When Wigman's company toured America in 1931, Holm found herself in the New World, where she promulgated the meaning of modern German dance and especially the emotional experience with which such dance actually started.

In this period, the stress in both ballet and modern dance in America was on indigenous spirit and folklore. Holm could have been a mere foreign interloper, but, as John Martin commented, her innate gentleness and humility marked her interest in allowing the vitality and freshness of the new land to lead her art to maturity. Gradually, she established herself as a choreographer of stature — particularly with *Trend* in 1937, which Sorell says created "a kind of heroic choric drama in which for words are substituted movement and a kind of dramatic expressionism." There was (in her own words) "a continuous change of weight, of volume, of linear and dimensional values." The dramatic character of *Trend* was a departure from the usual abstract symbolic handling of dance themes: spatial composition used planes and levels in long, sustained sweeps; and there was an "architectural" handling of light and colour in everything — from the lights to the floor cloth, from the cyclorama to the covering of the set.

Holm also tried her skill at surrealistic dance (*The Golden Fleece*, 1941) before venturing into musicals. Her most momentous success in this area was in *Kiss Me, Kate* (1948), where the dances were, in Sorell's words, "individually profiled and effervescent, demanding great skill without ever suggesting a muscle- flexing contest. They had the rare gift of making each dancer look as if he had a purpose in what he was doing." The range of dance forms used included classical ballet, jitterbug, soft-shoe, acrobatics, court and folk dance.

The Lerner and Loewe musical was to be her next great success, even though there was nothing in either the Shavian original or Lerner's script that encouraged anything but light terpsichorean content. Moreover, she was supposed to coach Holloway, who remembers telling her, "Now, don't try and teach me to dance, because I can't." However, she skilfully blended English music-hall steps and her own choreography. Loewe's music did provide occasions for intimacy, comedy, and drama, and the essential fidelity of the musical to Shaw's didactic art prompted a pure, clean style that used emotions as a stimulus to movement and form, and that stripped away artificiality in order to keep close to real life.

In November public auditions began for dancers and singers. Franz Allers, a Czechoslovakian émigré who had wielded the baton for the New York Philharmonic, the Philadelphia orchestra, for *Rodeo* at the Met, *Plain and Fancy* at the Hellinger, and for every Lerner and Loewe show since *The Day before Spring*, supervised the vocal auditions. After two weeks he reduced the number of hopefuls to approximately two hundred. After Loewe joined him (the two used German in their consultations) and cut that number down in half, Hart, Lerner, Levin, Beaton, and Holm lent their combined opinions for the final choices. While the musicians focused specifically on vocal ability and appearance, Holm studied the dancers' movements, Beaton scrutinized them for grace and an ability to wear his costumes, and Levin tried to determine if his salary offers would be accepted by those who made the final cut.

All the major roles, except one, had been cast. Robert Coote, one of Harrison's close professional friends, accepted the role of Pickering and seemed to be a wonderful foil in personality for Harrison. Philippa Bevans was to play Mrs. Pearce, Leo Britt would essay Zoltan Karpathy, Viola Roache would be Mrs. Eynsford-Hill, and Michael King (son of Dennis King, an outstanding musical comedy leading man) would have a go at Freddy. But the part of Mrs. Higgins, a pivotal one as far as Higgins's psychology was concerned, had not been set. Both Beaton and Hart wanted Cathleen Nesbitt, renowned character actress who had been Rupert Brooke's great love before his untimely death, and who had played everything from Shakespeare to Wilde to Bagnold. Lerner recounts that Hart called her and delivered a most bewitching invitation: "Cathleen, the role of Mrs. Higgins was never a great role and it is even smaller in the musical version. Furthermore, I want you to know it will not get any bigger and might even become smaller on the road. But we want you very much. Cecil has designed some ravishing clothes, you will look beautiful and you will receive your usual salary. Also, Cathleen, I beg you to consider this. For years now you have been appearing in very large roles in very bad plays, to which all your friends have come out of loyalty and suffered through the evening. I believe they will have a very good time at this play and I think you owe it to them to give them a nice evening in the theatre." Nesbitt was lured without further ado.

Work continued on the score. After sixteen months of work, Lerner and Loewe were still three important songs short of a complete score. Moss Hart had another worry: Lerner had not yet finished the book. It is generally agreed that of a musical's three important elements — book, music, lyrics — the book is the most important. As Martin Gottfried has remarked, "The book or text of a musical is the basis of the show's existence. . . . It is what the music and lyrics and dances are set to. It is the reason a musical is produced in the first place. Ultimately, it is the reason a show succeeds or fails."

Lerner could not satisfy Hart by assurances that the play and any alterations were all in his head. Hart ordered Lerner to accompany him to Atlantic City where the book would have to be completed before they ever would return to New York. Lerner protested that by his own estimate he would need only three more days' work. "Good," Lerner remembers being told by Hart. "You will do them in Atlantic City."

Actually, the enterprise took four days, but at the end of these, the men returned to New York rested and ready for the next business.

By the first week in December, Lerner and Loewe had "Get Me to the Church on Time" to accompany Doolittle's "With a Little Bit o' Luck." Both numbers sounded strongly like something out of old English variety, and Holloway loved them the moment he heard them. They had infectious rhythms, lusty humour, and seemed particularly apt for his style of vocalizing. Then the composers knocked off "I've Grown Accustomed to Her Face," which had beauty and simplicity, and which was an acting *tour de force* for Harrison, and then the duo finally managed Eliza's big song, "I

Could Have Danced All Night." Actually the title came first to Lerner who gave it to Loewe who then set the melody in a day. Lerner's lyric followed in twenty-four hours, though not completely to his own satisfaction, because there was, he felt, a certain "earthbound" quality. One line in particular made him blush in embarrassment: "And all at once my heart took flight." As he confessed in his memoir: "I have a special loathing for lyrics in which the heart is meta-morphosized and skips or leaps or jumps or 'takes flight.'" But no matter how he tinkered with it, he was never able to alter the line satisfactorily — which was especially galling to him when the song became the biggest popular hit that he and Loewe ever wrote.

Rehearsals and Try-Outs

ON 3 JANUARY 1956 rehearsals began officially at the New Amsterdam Roof, a shabby space that had once enjoyed a glittering reputation and glamour as the place where the world-famous Ziegfeld Follies used to reign. The dancing ensemble had already met and rehearsed a week earlier, and Harrison and Holloway had turned up in New York several weeks ahead to discuss their roles. But Julie Andrews, who as yet had no sense of being a star or of an obligation to a show, was making her very first appearance before the company. She had dispatched a letter to the producers, saying that she would arrive from London on the day rehearsals began, not earlier, because she was taking her two little brothers to a Christmas pantomime. Her attitude, according to biographer Richard Windeler, was "so different, so unbelievably unprofessional," that the producers were amused, rather than annoyed.

Chairs were arranged on stage for the entire company, and around the edges Moss Hart had laid out costume and set sketches. The press was admitted for interviews but only for about an hour, after which the reporters were asked to leave so that members of the company could get down as a unit to their business. Principals sat in the first row, secondary characters in the second, and the ensemble at the rear. Moss Hart sat stage centre at a desk, flanked by Beaton, Levin, Smith, Allers, Holm, Loewe, stage managers, and various assistants. Hart read the stage directions while the cast read their parts aloud. The usual custom at first readings is for actors to merely mumble their lines, feel their way tentatively through parts, and not deliver full-throated or full-spirited readings. However, this first reading was different. As Cecil Beaton recorded in a diary: ". . . everyone was keyed up, convinced that they were participating in something exciting. Each number was spontaneously applauded. The atmosphere was electric."

In his autobiography, *Act One*, Moss Hart recalled the special quality, alluding to the fact that only twice in his experience had stars given "as brilliant a performance at the first reading as they subsequently gave on stage. . . . Gertrude Lawrence, at the first reading of *Lady in the Dark*, and Rex Harrison, at the first reading of *My Fair Lady*, plunged into their parts with an electric excitement, from the first line onward, that was contagious enough to make their own excitement spread through the rest of the cast like a forest fire; it made this usually dispiriting experience a thing to be set apart and remembered with gratitude."

Lerner's recollection, however, was different — at least from the second act on: "The enthusiasm continued throughout the second act, except Rex's. His face grew longer and longer and his voice softer and softer. I knew exactly why. Somehow Higgins had gotten lost in the second act and because his is the central story, I felt his concern was justified." Harrison clearly needed another song in this act. But what?

On the way to a dinner engagement with Harrison at the Pierre Hotel that evening, Lerner thought back to a week earlier when the two men, while strolling down Fifth Avenue, had reviewed their sorry marital difficulties. Harrison had suddenly stopped and said in a loud voice that attracted public attention: "Alan! Wouldn't it be marvellous if we were homosexuals?" This was remarkably out of character for an actor who was reputed to be homophobic and a real ladies' man, and Lerner revolved the comment in his mind till he came up with the idea for "Why Can't a Woman Be More Like a Man?" (later re-titled "A Hymn to Him"). "It seemed a perfect second act vehicle through which Higgins could release his rage against Eliza for leaving him."

Harrison's temperament was to remain a problem throughout rehearsals and try-outs, but his immense comedic talent and vocal technique offset his impatience and egotistical outbursts. Julie Andrews, however, was clearly out of her depth. Moss Hart met her for the first time at rehearsal, and found her charming but without a clue about her part. By the fifth day, he got really terrified that she was not going to survive. Andrews told friends that she thought she knew what he wanted, but that every time she tried to do it, "something comes up in front of me and I'm like a crab clawing at a glass wall with Moss on the other side."

Andrews had a disconcerting habit of walking into the theatre while practising scales at top voice, and her clumsy acting and nervous habit of laughing in his face during dramatic scenes worsened Harrison's negative attitude to her. Gene Lees, author of *Inventing Champagne: The Worlds of Lerner and Loewe*, relates that Harrison once stormed out of rehearsals, threatening: "If this bitch is here on Monday, I'm quitting the show."

After the first four rehearsals, on the way home with his wife, Kitty Carlisle, Hart was unusually silent. Finally, according to Carlisle, he asked, "What do you think of Julie?"

"She needs a bit of help," his wife answered.

"Yes," he agreed, and then, as if musing, he added, "If I were David Belasco I would take Julie to a hotel for the weekend. I'd never let her out; I'd order up room service. I'd keep her there and *paste* the part on her."

"Why don't you do it?" his wife urged.

Lees recounts how Hart didn't take Andrews to a hotel, but instead dismissed the company for two full days and took her to the New Amsterdam Theater. There, sealed off from prying eyes (except for those of Miles Kreuger, a young actor who became one of Lerner's assistants), the director and his young actress put the part of Eliza together bit by bit. Hart was to recall: "It was the sort of thing you couldn't do in front of a company without destroying a human being. We met in this silent, lonely, dark theatre, and I told her, 'Julie, this is stolen time, time I can't really afford. So there can be no time for politeness and you mustn't take offence, because there aren't any second chances in the theatre. There isn't time to do the whole Actors Studio bit. We have to start from the first line and go over the play line by line."

They worked seven hours daily, and Hart lit into her: "You're playing this like a Girl Guide. . . . You're not thinking, you're just oozing out the scene. . . . You're gabbling."

Andrews felt bullied, cajoled, and coaxed by this Svengali, but she was ever grateful to him for forcing her to be Eliza. At the time, "He made me infuriated, and scared and mad and frightened and in awe and full of an inferiority complex, while knowing I could do it, he worked and worked on me. I really did need a strong guiding hand. It was such a big musical and I had so little courage. I didn't know what Eliza should be, a whiny girl or a gutsy girl, a weak character or a strong one. Moss supplied the route, and as the nights went by, I absorbed Eliza more and more."

Secret voyeur, Miles Kreuger, was amazed at the transformation, though he credited Andrews for her innate talent and determination: "All I can tell you is that Julie Andrews had it all in there, way down deep somewhere, because it was like lifting the veils. And two days later, when rehearsals resumed, Julie Andrews was, full-blown, the Julie Andrews we know today — that uninhibited, wonderful comedienne who can give so much and do screwball things, do everything."

Kitty Carlisle Hart observed that for about three weeks she could hear every inflection of her husband in Andrews's reading of the lines, but she also noted that Andrews "had the wit and the talent to make the part her own."

Moss Hart was also impressed: "She was neither affronted nor hurt. She was delighted. We were both absolutely done in. But she made it. She has that terrible English strength that makes you wonder why they lost India."

Yet, it was by no means a settled issue. No great role ever is. Technical and emotional challenges remain throughout the run of a show, and the muses often fail to inspire performers, no matter how well-rehearsed and technically proficient they are. Andrews and Hart used to have fifteen-minute refresher courses in the powder room of the theatre, while the rest of the cast continued with rehearsals. She found the long dialogue scenes difficult, as well as the gutter quality of the Covent Garden Eliza. She had learned her Cockney from an American, Alfred Dixon, a former actor who had become a dialect teacher and who had, he claimed, all the world's speech inflections as if he were a vocational cousin of Higgins. At first, the Cockney used in the musical was too authentic for American audiences, and had to be toned down considerably. Andrews recalled: "The trouble with the dialect was that it varied slightly between men and women, and between that in use today and in the period of the play, which is Edwardian. In those days men were different: their voices were deep and low, and the women's were shriller and sort of high."

Another difficulty was the singing itself. For her entire run in the show (two years on Broadway, eighteen months in London), she was never certain, on any given night, that she would have enough strength to do the whole part flat out. "I found it an enormous weight every night and I can't remember a single performance when I didn't wonder to myself: 'Am I going to get through it tonight?' and 'I'll have to save myself a little in this song so that I have enough voice left for my next number.' It was such an enormous show — the screaming, the singing purely, the singing 'on the chest,' the great dramatic requirements."

Andrews endeared herself to the company in general and to the British contingent in particular by brewing tea backstage for herself and compatriots. Stanley Holloway had announced during the first week of rehearsals that he couldn't continue without his afternoon cup of tea, and Moss Hart allowed him, Harrison, Andrews, and Nesbitt to observe their national custom.

All the while, Hart kept the company in good spirits, arriving each day with fresh jokes. He was a judicious director who knew that a big production generated big tensions, and he recognized that part of his job was to be a diplomat seeking peaceful co-existence. Harrison's continuing egotism had to be given its vent, but there had to be some light relief.

Harrison was ever-conscious of his star billing, but his ego was under duress by the very fact of this being his first musical. In *A Damned Serious Business*, Harrison says that he knew that he was risking his considerable reputation "for a certain, very particular kind of comedy acting, to do something [he] didn't know [he] could do." To foster confidence in him, Hart devoted evening rehearsals during the first week entirely to Higgins. This form of attention did not please Stanley Holloway, who sat in his room at the Algonquin, feeling rather despondent. One night he decided he was not going to take any more of this. He called up Herman Levin, and after declaring his unhappiness, said that he was giving them three weeks to find a replacement. Staggered by this, Levin froze. "I feel absolutely out of it," Holloway explained. "Nobody seems to bother about me or my part. Nobody even says 'Good morning' when I arrive at the theatre."

After a long pause, Levin pleaded: "Look, will you let me handle this my way?"

The next morning when Holloway arrived at rehearsal, he was bid cheery "good mornings" from all sides, and he burst into laughter. Then Moss Hart took him off into a corner and said, "I am rehearsing a girl who has never played a major role in her life, and an actor who has never sung on the stage in his life. You have done both. If you feel neglected, it is a compliment." There was no more talk from Holloway, he admits, about quitting the show.

Harrison continued, however, to dominate proceedings. His song, "A Hymn to Him," interrupted one of the best scenes of his friend, Robert Coote — the one where Pickering calls the Home Office to complain about Eliza's disappearance — and, according to Lees, Rex admitted later that for a long time their friendship was "strained." He annoyed Cecil Beaton by his excessive complaints about the minutest details of costuming, prompting Beaton to record: "Rex is like a dog with a rat and will 'worry' details at enormous length. If given the opportunity, he will work himself up into a state of nervous alarm. I cannot say that Rex is the easiest boy in the class.... One morning, he ripped off in anger his first-act long coat because it was tight under the arms." Then, one evening after dinner at Beaton's, he suddenly decided that he did not want to play the role of Higgins. "They wanted Gielgud — they'd better get him," remembers Beaton in *The Restless Years*. All this was ego exercise, but there was also a deep-rooted fear of failure. Knowing full well that his career was at an important crossroads, he wanted to ensure success. He would rehearse his lyrics so often that the rest of the company was worn down. "The chorus-girls, long since exhausted, lay on the floor or were sprawled in the stalls, while Rex repeated, over and over again, certain phrases of 'I've Grown Accustomed To Her Face.' At length, when he was playing the last-act fight scene with Liza and she threw the slippers hard in his face, the entire chorus applauded from the stalls."

Despite these *frissons*, Harrison had undisputed taste and style as a performer. He wanted to be true to Shaw, and his chief worry at the beginning of the enterprise was that the lyrics might not match Shaw's dialogue in *Pygmalion*. He also did not want the show to sacrifice any of Shaw's witty rhetoric, so he zealously carried around a Penguin edition of *Pygmalion* in his pocket, referring to it frequently, and interrupting Hart to argue every point. He appeared to have become Higgins, intent on defending the English language against "barbaric" Americans. It seemed to Lerner that Harrison referred to his Penguin edition "At least four times a day," and "if a speech did not seem right to him, he would cry out: 'Where's my Penguin?' " After about a week of this, Lerner purchased a stuffed penguin from a taxidermist, and the next time Harrison yelled, "Where's my Penguin?" the stuffed one was rolled out from the wings — to the uproarious laughter of the cast and Harrison. There were no more calls for the Penguin, and "the stuffed edition" remained in Harrison's dressing room "as a mascot throughout the run of the production."

By his own admission, Lerner did make "one grave error." When Harrison marvelled at one of Higgins's speeches after "The Rain in Spain" number and asked him "Where in Shaw did you find it?" Lerner told the truth: "I wrote it." Harrison suddenly lost respect for the passage and seldom got it right in rehearsal. Ever after, if Harrison asked of a line, "Is that yours?" Lerner would always claim to have found it somewhere in Shaw — perhaps in "one of Shaw's letters or in a preface or an essay. That seemed to satisfy him and [there were] no more difficulties."

Towards the second week of rehearsal, the musical finally found its title. Herman Levin had the layout for the first newspaper advertisement — for the New Haven opening night — and this announced: "Herman Levin presents Rex Harrison and Julie Andrews in '?' " Levin made an urgent appeal for a working title: "Call it anything.

You can always change it on the road. After all, when *Oklahoma!* opened it was called 'Away We Go.' " Lerner suggested that the title should be a compromise — "the title that we all dislike the least." Harrison says that after a "collective, apathetic nod," and a brief rundown of all the choices, the title deemed to be "the least indigestible" was *My Fair Lady*, with the possessive "*My*" stressing "the dominating masculine angle," and the phrase being a Cockney pun on "Mayfair Lady," and a phrase derived from the children's chant, "London Bridge Is Falling Down." Frederick Loewe, according to his partner, however, remained loyal to *Fanfaroon*.

There was one more major controversy before the New Haven opening, and this concerned "Without You," which Julie Andrews sang near the end of the play. Rex Harrison made it very clear that he was not going to stand up on stage "like an idiot doing nothing" while Andrews sang the whole number at him. He did not object to the song or its content — Eliza's triumphant liberation from Higgins — but he felt upstaged and foolishly immobile. Lerner and Loewe panicked, but Moss Hart remained calm, deciding to do nothing until everything else in the play was rehearsed. The final run-through (with the omission of "Without You") went well. On the train to New Haven, Lerner recounts how Hart sat next to Harrison and used gentle firmness: "Rex. Julie is going to sing 'Without You' in that scene whether you are on the stage or not. It is my personal opinion you will look like a horse's ass if you leave the stage when she begins it and return when she has finished. However, if you will give me the opportunity, I will show you how it can be staged."

The first rehearsal Moss Hart arranged in New Haven was for the Andrews song, and the company waited anxiously to see whether Harrison would walk off or even appear at all. But he ended the suspense by showing up and approving of Hart's new staging. The clever solution was to give Higgins two verses to be done at the end of Eliza's song, in which he reacts delightedly to her new-found independence:

By George, I really did it
I did it. I did it.

I said I'd make a woman
And indeed I did.

I knew that I could do it!
I knew it! I knew it!
I said I'd made an woman
And succeed I did!

Higgins reaffirmed his Pygmalion arrogance, and deflected attention away from her ecstasy to his own chauvinistic rhyming brio. The repetitive phrases, set in a brisk staccato of consonance, allowed his dynamism and sharp assertiveness to top her celebration. And the quick tempo recalled the tango rhythm of "The Rain in Spain," where Eliza was spontaneously and briefly allowed to be an equal partner with Higgins and Pickering in a peak of sheer blissful accomplishment.

The orchestra accompaniment for the whole show was still relatively new, and there was a general buzz of excitement as Franz Allers conducted his thirty-two musicians through Loewe's romantic, cheerful, dramatic score. As the tunes were played through, with sometimes operatic grandeur, the company ovation itself grew operatic. But there was a disconcerting wrinkle in the excitement — and once again it was caused by Rex Harrison. Harrison recalls that during pre-orchestra rehearsals, Julie Andrews used to encourage him by saying, "Just wait until you get the orchestra, it's like a marvellous sort of eiderdown, you can relax into it." That was true if you were a genuine singer, but he was a song-talker. Kitty Carlisle Hart had forewarned him: "Rex, at the first orchestra rehearsal you'll be quite disoriented. It's a terrible hazard even for experienced performers. So far you've only sung with piano, and you can always hear the melody. With full orchestra, you'll hear everything *but* the melody. You won't even find your first note, much less anything else. Don't panic. It will eventually sort itself out."

As she had predicted, he was thrown off, fell out of good countenance, panicked, and raged. Unable to pause for a laugh, as he could in a straight play, because the orchestra went straight on without him, he was absolutely lost. He became even more in terror of the orchestra than usual. Franz Allers had kept the orchestra down for him in certain places, and had demarcated a clarinet as the instrument to carry the melodies as the star just thought and talked his songs through. But Harrison was still flustered and insecure. According to Lees, Allers tried to coax him into sitting next to him and being taken through the numbers slowly: "We have hardly thirty minutes of music to go and we have two and a half hours." Moss Hart promised Harrison that he could rehearse alone with the orchestra in front of the house curtain for as long as he needed, Harrison remembers. At four in the afternoon of the opening, the star sent word from his dressing room that he would not perform that night. Special entreaties were made to get him to change his mind, but, according to Hart, he was adamant: "I never *liked* musical com, and I won't *do* musical com!" He locked himself in his room, partly out of rage, and partly out of terror. So Hart had little choice but to dismiss the company and crew, and have his brother, Bernie, the show's assistant manager, place hourly radio bulletins announcing cancellation of the performance.

The weather had turned dramatically inclement, and at five o'clock, the manager of the Shubert Theatre confronted Lerner, Loewe, Hart, and Levin in the lobby: "There's a raging blizzard outside. People from miles around have already left their houses to mush through to the theatre. I can't head them all off even if I get on the radio now. There will be a riot in this lobby at seven-thirty when I announce that there won't be any performance." He had no choice, Lees claims, but to put all the blame on Rex Harrison.

As the lobby filled with people bubbling with excitement over the anticipated opening, agents rushed to Harrison's dressing room to negotiate. "I can't open. I just cannot open," the star held firmly. He was told it would be a scandal if he didn't go on. "Listen, I'm not ready," he countered. "I will go on if I have to, but I'm not ready to do it, *I am not ready to do it!*"

The Shubert line, Lees relates, was: "You can't do this, it's unprofessional. We'll be letting down a regular audience, an audience that keeps this theatre going, year after year, when you are not here to care, and it's they and us who'll suffer long after you've moved on." There would be no option but to blame the débacle on Harrison. His own agent pounded on the door: "Come out! Come out! You'll never work again, Rex! You've got to do this!"

An hour before the curtain, Harrison emerged from his room, but the company had already been dismissed and had long since dispersed in various directions. To Bernie Hart fell the unenviable task of re-gathering the company. He went to all the cinemas in the vicinity, asking that the shows be interrupted so that he could yell, "Everybody from the *Fair Lady* company back to the theater; we're opening tonight!" Then he moved on to health-clubs and made the same announcement: "People were jumping off massage tables, flinging their sheets onto the floor, and heading for the theater. By the time the curtain went up, not one member of the company was missing," his wife remembers.

At eight-forty, the curtain rose to a sold-out house. The first act ran twenty-five minutes too long, and there were technical difficulties — the electrical turntables rotated slowly and some of the curtains got fouled. Holloway lifted the show with his boisterous number, but "Come to the Ball" was, as Lerner recalled, "a disaster in three-quarter time" and "On the Street Where You Live" was greeted with "mute disinterest." But suddenly in the second act everything smoothened out, and the cast was thrilled to find the audience palpably *listening*. By the reprise of "On the Street," while he was crossing backstage, Holloway knew that "this show was going to be a world wonder, and that its numbers would be whistled, hummed, sung and danced to all over the world for years." At the final curtain, the audience stood and cheered, and a warm flush of success showed on the faces of all the cast.

The general elation was not shared by Cecil Beaton, however, who was still livid with rage because Julie Andrews had not pulled her hat forward during "Show Me." "That bitch!" he fumed, quite oblivious to the fact that Eliza had merely followed instructions from Hart and Lerner who had not wanted her face covered while she sang. Beaton was true to his almost egomaniacal form, virtually assuming that he was a Pygmalion to Andrews. Arrogant and snobbish, he sometimes rivalled Harrison for temperamental outbursts, brooking criticism with less enthusiasm than most other creative people. Kitty Carlisle Hart, who called him "a minor genius," recalled a dress rehearsal when she thought Eliza's costume for the Ball "most unbecoming," and was on the verge of saying so, when she was quickly hushed by Oliver Smith who whispered, "Don't even shake your head — Cecil is right behind us." When Beaton asked her later if she liked Eliza's dress, she replied tersely, "No, Cecil," and he didn't speak to her for three days, though he did redesign the costume very successfully.

Kitty was in bed with the flu during the New Haven opening, and when she made a phone call to her husband to ask how it had gone, Hart answered, according to Lees, in a somewhat subdued tone, "It's some kind of a hit. I don't know how big." The next morning discussions were held about cuts for Act 1, and about how to address the problem of "On the Street Where You Live." Everyone, except Lerner, wanted to drop the song from the show. Loewe had never particularly cared for it, but Lerner "liked the melody and thought the flagrantly romantic lyric that kept edging on the absurd exactly right for the character." The matter lay unresolved until two or three days later when it occurred to him that the audience was probably baffled by the placement of the song and by the singer's costume: "[B]ecause it was sung immediately following the Ascot scene, and Freddy Eynsford-Hill was dressed exactly the same as all the other gentlemen at Ascot, perhaps the audience did not realize he was the same boy who had been sitting next to Eliza and talking to her during the scene." The solution was to change the verse before the main chorus and replace "the flowery, romantic one he was then singing with one that echoed Eliza at Ascot. . . . Fritz changed the music accordingly . . . [and] on Thursday night 'On the Street Where You Live' almost required an encore," recounts Lerner in his 1978 book *The Street Where I Live*.

To trim the first act down to size, they cut "Come to the Ball," a ballet between Ascot and the Embassy Ball, and "Say a Prayer for Me Tonight." In the first instance, Harrison's cheerful number to console a woebegone Eliza after the Ascot epoch-making gaffe, there was a dream-ballet where the male chorus enacted various chores, such as doing up Eliza's hair, teaching her to dance, preparing her costume, et cetera. Then Harrison danced with her and exited with the boys, leaving Julie Andrews on stage with Mrs. Pearce, the housekeeper, to sing "Say a Prayer." Superficially, there was nothing wrong with this scene, for as Stanley Holloway observed, "it was nicely dressed and had colour and grace and movement and just the right touch of sentiment. In fact, it might well have been the highlight of many other musicals." But Stanley Holloway recalls that Lerner, Loewe, and Hart "somehow knew that, for all its trappings, it was a phoney. To them it stood out gratingly like a piece of costume jewellery in Cartier's window." ("It later emerged from the trunk and was used in *Gigi*," according to Lerner.) Lerner substituted a brief scene "which skipped directly from Ascot to the night before the ball." When Moss Hart read this alteration very slowly and carefully, he looked at Lerner and exclaimed: "You son of a bitch! How dare you give me an inferiority complex?" The new scene also solved a major costume problem: by showing off Eliza's Embassy Ball gown at the top of the stairs in Higgins's home, rather than in the extraordinary parade of glamour at the Ball itself, the show was able to obtain a stunning isolated effect and win a thunderous ovation as a tiara-crested Eliza descended the stairs to the music of "I Could Have Danced All Night," while Higgins and Pickering looked on admiringly in their elegant Edwardian evening clothes.

Philadelphia was next on the itinerary. The four weeks there at the Erlanger Theater were spent, remembers Lerner, "polishing the performances, sharpening a line here, an exit there, making the technical production flow efficiently, and completing the lighting." One night, Lerner and Loewe tried to improve "You Did It" (which opens the second act), by fixing a section in the middle which lacked a proper climax. In it Higgins was recounting to the servants Eliza's success at the ball and how Karpathy, a rival phoneticist, had concluded that she was not only a princess, but a Hungarian one, at that. Lerner amended it as follows: "I know each language on the map, said he, / And she's Hungarian as the first Hungarian rhapsody." Harrison loved the lines, rehearsed them, then completely forgot every lyric in the show the night he had to sing the new lines. This set off another of his screaming rages, as he stabbed a finger at Lerner and shouted: "Don't you dare do that to me again!" There was no other recourse but to remove the two new lines.

Harrison had another problem during the Philadelphia run. This came about as a result of a spectacular scenic effect when three elaborate chandeliers descended during the finale of Act I, producing "a collective orgasm" of ecstasy in the audience. Lowered a little too far one night, one of them snagged itself on his hairpiece, and when a stagehand tried correcting the error and raising the delinquent chandelier, the star's hair flew up with it. Retaining his composure, Harrison continued as if nothing untoward had occurred, though the audience could see the hairpiece "hanging from a chandelier like a bird's nest after a storm." At the end of the act, Harrison was fit to be tied. He demanded that the guilty stagehand be brought before him, but Lees says that Phil Adler, the stage manager, refused: "No, Rex, I won't bring him here. He's a brute. You'll insult him and he'll kill you." Harrison raved to Moss Hart on the telephone, but resumed his performance in the second act.

While the first act in Philadelphia had become the stuff of theatrical anecdote because of a chandelier's mischief with a hairpiece, the second act became memorialized later in the run because of what Lerner calls "one of the loudest farts ever heard in the history of theater." In the fourth scene, set in Mrs. Higgins's winter garden, Harrison suddenly had an uncomfortable urge to break wind. He managed to control himself until he had some business behind the flowerpots where, while pacing irritably in character, he relieved his pressure. However, he had miscalculated the force and volume, emitting an unmistakably vulgar sound. The audience "behaved beautifully," even as Cathleen Nesbitt as Mrs. Higgins remonstrated: "Henry, dear. Please don't grind your teeth." A full minute later, however, when he moved downstage to Eliza and said, "My manners are the same as Colonel Pickering's," the audience burst out into massive laughter. The sound built like huge waves and rolled through the house, and (as Lerner recalled) "like 'Ol' Man River' it kept rollin' right through the entire scene and into the next."

Advance word-of-mouth began building during the New Haven and Philadelphia runs. The out-of-town notices had trumpeted Julie Andrews as the next big Broadway star, Rex Harrison as a genuine theatre deity, and the show itself as the apogee of musical theatre up to that point. In New York, mail orders for advance tickets were voluminous. The Mark Hellinger box-office opened two weeks before the Broadway première, and daily queues formed like long necklaces around the block. And yet it was impossible to predict what the ultimate fate of *My Fair Lady* would be. Lerner nervously doubted that any show could live up to such massive expectations. Lees says that Julie Andrews was coolly cautious: "We still haven't opened in New York." The New York critical "gods" had not yet sat in judgement, and pre-Broadway runs were merely try-outs before the big time finals. New Haven and Philadelphia had given the producers two chances to improve the show. The upcoming opening in the Big Apple would be the ultimate test.

Show curtain by Oliver Smith.

Oliver Smith's design for the Tottenham
Court Road tenement setting.

Oliver Smith's set design for Higgins's study on Wimpole Street, showing part of revolve on the right.

Oliver Smith's scene painting for Drury Lane.

*Eliza reacts with terrified suspicion as Higgins
makes notes on her Cockney pronunciation.*

Eliza with violets at Covent Garden.

Higgins remonstrates against allowing women in his life.

Eliza is forced to use marbles in her
mouth in order to improve her diction.

Pickering and Higgins are amazed by Doolittle.

Eliza and Higgins celebrate her elocutionary success by dancing to a tango rhythm in the "Rain in Spain" number.

*Pickering and Higgins play matador and bull
around Eliza in the "Rain in Spain" number.*

Eliza, seated between an adoring Freddy and an amused
Mrs. Higgins, makes a startling impression at Ascot.

Eliza (at Ascot), with Pickering on her right
and Mrs. Higgins on her left, yells out,
"Come on, Dover!!! Move your bloomin' arsse!!!"

Eliza and Higgins prepare for the Embassy Ball.

Opening Night on Broadway

EXTRA POLICE WERE ON DUTY outside the Mark Hellinger Theatre on the evening of 15 March 1956, as glistening limousines delivered opening-night patrons, resplendent in formal evening wear, and as masses of onlookers thronged the vicinity. The cast and crew were confident of at least a three-month run because the theatre had been bought out for that period by various charities. Besides, the New Haven and Philadelphia runs had built confidence within the company, although everyone knew that Broadway musicals were an expensive form of gambling. Moreover, for the superstitious, there was some real concern that the two immediate predecessors at the Hellinger had failed badly, and since jinxes usually came in threes, would *My Fair Lady* prove to be the third successive failure at this theatre?

Not having had a genuinely big Broadway hit since *Brigadoon* in 1947, Alan J. Lerner had quietly sipped champagne with his second wife, Nancy Olson, before escorting her to the theatre. As she slipped into a seat near a friend, Lerner, as was his custom, paced anxiously back and forth at the rear, watching the audience intently, covering (by his own estimate) two miles in his nervous exercise. In his book on Loewe and Lerner, Lees recounts that almost a year earlier, his wife had remarked sadly to her husband's Harvard friend, Ben Welles: "Oh, Ben, he needs a hit so badly! He really needs it."

Frederick Loewe was a total contrast in manner and attitude to Lerner. He had a self-confidence that defied the odds. In 1934, when he had played piano in the pit for Kitty Carlisle in *Champagne Sec* (a version of *Die Fledermaus*), he would visit her dressing room every evening while she was making up and say in his strong Viennese lilt: "Someday I'm going to wrrrite the best musical of Brroadway,"

Carlisle remembers. His opening night behaviour this March was relatively calm. Usually, he was "an in-and-outer," walking out for a cigarette during the dialogue and returning when the music began. Now he was "the picture of satisfaction," according to his partner.

The tumult outside the theatre at first seemed to offset the audience's reaction during the first act. People sat hushed, "staring too hard at the stage to see anything," "listening too intently to hear anything." To Lerner, it seemed as if "they had all gathered for the second coming of Christ and He was late."

The overture sparkled with its brisk, racing strings, then becoming sweepingly romantic. Because of the shallowness of the Hellinger stage, Oliver Smith had had to rely on false perspective to augment the sense of space, and his scene painting impressively pulled together suggestions of religion, commerce, and art through décor of church, pillars, opera house, and Covent Garden flower-market. The colour scheme and lighting were first dark, with buskers from the old days seen huddled over smudgepot fires in a living tableau of a now-vanished era. This was (what Walter Kerr recalled) "a blithe little October-night idyll, with Liza being given a friendly ride in a garbage can" while a number of her friends, with brooms over their shoulders, skipped out a few Hanya Holm steps. It was obvious from the outset that this musical would not make choreography a focal point, though it would never blur the focus on *movement* or *rhythm*. Everyone on stage seemed to have *purposeful movement* or the illusion of such, whether huddling together, leaning on a broomstick, cavorting in Cockney glee, slouching against a pillar, or pushing Eliza around in a cart.

The street entertainers in the dark bustling opening drew little laughter, though the audience appreciated the sight of glass-roof pavilions opening to the weather, and the parade of resplendently-garbed opera guests moving into a burst of rain. The first scene suddenly expanded into a glorious setpiece, with Moss Hart's direction managing to be compact yet brisk, as it maintained a firm composition of group movements and emphasized principals.

Julie Andrews, in her mud-stained boots, smudged face, and dark boater, was a howling savage, yet her confrontation with a tan and beige Rex Harrison drew only modest laughter. The songs (particularly Higgins's "Why Can't the English?") were well-applauded, but far from indicative of a mega-hit. Andrews sounded nice chest tones as she sang with what Thomas R. Dash called "dulcet sweetness," and there was a vivid vocal contrast between this slumming Galatea and her irascibly precise Pygmalion who sang, however, rather like a failed thespian in a shower. Robert Coote's stuffy Pickering had not yet had enough time to register his silly-ass comedy, and the first scene came across amiably enough, with just adequate flair to keep the audience interested, if not fully beguiled.

Lerner looked at Loewe and saw that his face did not register concern, but at the end of the scene, Moss Hart rushed over frantically to the pair. "I knew it. It's just a New Haven hit. That's all. Just a New Haven hit." Loewe smiled in sympathetic amusement, recalls Lerner, and said, "My darling Mossie, . . . If you don't know this is the biggest hit that has ever come to New York you had better come with me and get a drink." When they returned from the bar about five minutes later, Stanley Holloway's rendition of "With a Little Bit o' Luck" was bringing down the house. This song was set outside a pub in a Tottenham Court Road tenement setting, devised by Oliver Smith with a sort of Dickensian squalor. In traditional dustman's cap and string-tied trousers, Holloway galloped around as Lerner had described in the script, "equally free from fear and conscience," delighted by Eliza's gift of coin that could buy him and his two pals (played with fine spirit by Gordon Dilworth and Rod McLennan) some more glorious beer.

Scene three was a vivid contrast, with one of Oliver Smith's two revolves leading to Higgins's study in Wimple Street and an environment that breathed insulated pedantry and self-contained, self-glorifying technological gadgetry. A gas-lit room with no view other than of its own masculine busts, tuning forks of various sizes, recorders and speakers, filing cabinets, staircase and balconies. This was actually the very first design that Smith had done for the production, and it combined sculpture, architecture, and painting to underline one of Shaw's recurring themes of a private, coded world of intellectual and mechanical power but humanistic deficiency. In this male world, where the only discernible passion was Higgins's love of phonetics, Rex Harrison played all the scales available to his flexible tenor-baritone, his manner ranging from impetuosity to clever calculation, from genial bullying to stormy petulance, though at times he seemed to be condescending to Lerner's script, rather like a duke indulging a villager. It was here that the show, already palpably good, would take off.

Using Robert Coote's Pickering as an apt foil for his own unmalicious naughtiness, Harrison toyed with Andrews's "deliciously low — so horribly dirty" Eliza, laying down severe injunctions against idleness and wickedness, threatening her with decapitation, and offering only a very modest reward of "seven-and-six to start life with as a lady in a shop." To Coote's gravely anxious question, "Are you a man of good character where women are concerned?", Harrison smoothly parried: "Have you ever met a man of good character where women are concerned?" Then he dogmatically set forth his philosophy of "ordinariness" in an extraordinary fashion, making the scene the first truly electrifying one in the show. Taking his melodic cue from a solitary clarinet in Allers's orchestra, Harrison used gesture sparingly, but his sense of rhythm very grandly. He bounced off a chair to hunch his shoulders, elevated his eyebrows, wagged a finger mightily, threw up his right arm magisterially, and used a twangy, mordant, confident air to show just how slyly inaccurate the song's title was. Everything he did seemed to possess innate rhythm — his breathing, leaping, gesticulating, pausing, *and* slouching. "Mr. Harrison's slouch is a rhythmic slouch," effused Walter Kerr in his opening-night review. "His voice is a showman's voice. . . . His leaps over the fashionable furniture are the leaps of a true enthusiast. But most of all Mr. Harrison is an actor, he believes every cranky, snappish, exhilarating syllable of the Alan Jay Lerner lyric he is rattling off, and a fourteen-carat character simply crashes its way onto the stage."

Not to be outdone, Andrews had her own virtuosic moment minutes later with a sadly comic, sweetly furious fantasy solo. Unlike her first number ("Wouldn't It Be Loverly?"), this one showed a singer whose composure did not remain unruffled as she sang of suffering and revenge. Furious with Higgins for his relentless derision, nagging, and abuse, she gave vent to Eliza's pent-up anger, and showed that neither Mrs. Pat Campbell nor Gertrude Lawrence could ever have held a candle to her in the instant. Her eyes flashed, her jaw hardened, and the venom in her heart spewed forth in "Just You Wait." Walter Kerr accorded her an accolade: "Miss Andrews has caught you, too, now — she is funny, she is pathetic, she is savagely true. Eliza isn't just a doll, she's a demon with a soul you can understand."

But the indisputable climax of Act I — as far as the audience was concerned — came unexpectedly during one of her wearying elocution drills, after the chorus of servants had tried to squeeze sympathy for Higgins's persistent tutorials. Even those in a small minority who would later complain of a lack of a big explosive song, had to admit that the sheer dramatic surprise and forceful gaiety of "The Rain in Spain" number had a startling freshness and buoyant energy that elevated everybody's spirit at the Mark Hellinger. The tune began as the slightest rumour of an incipient celebration. After who knew how many ghastly errors, Eliza quietly and slowly got a sentence right — leading a leaden Higgins to revive from his torpor of disgust and Pickering to drop his English conservatism. Joy and victory fed into a racy tango beat, with crisp flamenco embroiderings, heel-clicking on sofa and floor, a wild jig, a mock bull-fight, and then total collapse back upon a sofa, with the trio overcome by laughter and relief.

Wolcott Gibbs deemed it "just about the most brilliantly successful scene" he had ever seen in a musical comedy. "It is a moment that has practically everything — charm, style, wit, gaiety — and I will cherish it as long as I live."

But after such glory, would the rest of the first act be an anti-climax? The question must have been on everyone's mind as the production moved, after Andrews's crystal-clear and soaring "I Could Have Danced All Night," to the sunny, stately elegance of Ascot. The grandstand white and the lawn of green nylon were a perfect background for Beaton's parade of showgirl hats and hobble skirts, men in grey frock-coats and silk hats, the whole picture a sophistication of black-grey-and-white. At the enclosure, the lords and ladies watched the off-stage races with sedate composure, facing the footlights in a long row and incarnating Lerner's satirical point that English upper-class reserve was as formalized and studied as a gavotte.

This interesting interpolation (it was pure Lerner, for not a jot came from Shaw here) was a means to shift Mrs. Higgins's At-Home tea to a box at Ascot, so that Eliza might achieve two very practical ends: prove that she could master proper diction for her début into high society, and impel Freddy to fall madly in love with her. Cathleen Nesbitt's Mrs. Higgins was breathtaking in a grey-and-orchid gown, whereas Julie Andrews's pink pleats and ruffles did not quite impart the sense of someone dressed just a shade too extravagantly to pull off her charade of upper-class dignity. She looked beautiful and charming, rather than ever-so-slightly off-key and comic, and it was possibly Cecil Beaton's only miscalculation. But Andrews more than compensated for this by her Cockney vulgarity at the track, sending the on-stage Ascot crowd into benumbing shock and a blackout, and the Mark Hellinger audience into guffaws as she cried out to her betting favourite: "Come on, Dover!!! Move your bloomin' arse!!!"

Beaton himself compensated Miss Andrews moments later by giving her a pink and silver Embassy Ball gown that, assisted by tiara and jewels and her own air, summed up the glamour of theatre. Her descent of a staircase was a strong enchantment, and Oliver Smith's double turntables spun round yet again for a chandelier-lit ballroom that earned loud, spontaneous applause from the audience. As Loewe's "Embassy Waltz" swirled and soared, dipped and rose, and the guests whirled as in a lavish operetta, My Fair Lady was well on its way to greatness.

In the second act, Robert Coote as Pickering came to the fore in one splendid scene that gave him an opportunity to be ridiculously expansive and slow-on-the-uptake. In Act 1 he had shown an unusual manly pride when serving as dressmaker's dummy for Eliza's first fancy gown. Now in the second act — with Eliza's bolting from Wimpole Street after the two men had ignored her crucial role in their Embassy triumph — he had a delicious scene registering blank shock, repeating his "Well, I'm dashed" three times, and turning this triple repetition into a magnification of his own expostulating helplessness. This was followed by a resolute telephone call to Scotland Yard that he began with sunny amiability before allowing clouds of trouble to scud across his face as he twitched his moustache as if to stimulate thought. Where Harrison had his slouch and swift spoken delivery, Coote had his moustache and air of ridiculous vacuity.

The rest was simply a consolidation of tone and style, with Holloway given one more show-stopper, "Get Me to the Church on Time," as he, accoutred in cutaway, top-hat, spats, and cummerbund, with a carnation in his lapel, prepared for his imminent wedding and new bourgeois life, and was borne aloft the shoulders of his wastrel friends, many of whom were resplendent in pearly button costumes. Hanya Holm's choreography gave the tatterdemalion Cockney ensemble a blaze of spins and whirls and a virtual can-can. Never swamping the mock-hymn melody by excessive business or rushed tempo, Holloway's avuncular but roguish charm made the moment delightfully credible, though more sentimental than Shaw might have preferred.

The second act laid on the romance with heaps of sentimentality. Freddy Eynsford-Hill, no more than an excuse by Shaw to make didactic points against Eliza's falling in love with Higgins, was played with stars-in-his-eyes by Michael King who once more sang Freddy's signature song, "On the Street Where You Live," like a chip off his famous father's block. Julie Andrews was in full bloom in the second-half, easily convincing the audience in the icily regal ballroom that she could subdue the Hungarian Karpathy's scepticism by her radiance, then revealing yet again a smouldering sense of wounded pride and fierce self-respect in her exchanges with Higgins. She launched into a defiant rendition of "Without You," set off by a finger-snapping in his face, and then exploded on the street at Freddy's indecisiveness ("Show Me").

Rex Harrison, who performed Higgins's pivotal solo ("I've Grown Accustomed to Her Face") before a drop-cloth of the street, drew attention to Lerner's clever way of altering Shaw's fable and fixing it with his own distinctive romantic logic. Harrison was able to move from impatient anger to chauvinist arrogance to fiendishly malicious fantasy to terrifying self-discovery all with lightning-swift but apparently effortless ease. He turned Higgins finally into a vulnerable human being, quite solitary and lost as he re-entered his Wimpole Street study in the blue-grey light of early evening. With slow, silent ruefulness, he turned on the machine by the door to play back Eliza's voice, and as Julie Andrews quietly re-emerged, her stillness being a curious suggestion of "the obedient reserve of the Galatea of Greek legend," she granted him the illusion of restored pride. Harrison played the finale with impeccable body rhythm, leaning back with a contented sigh, pushing his hat forward till it almost covered his face, and asking softly but joyously, "Eliza? Where the devil are my slippers?" as the curtain descended.

The ovation was thunderous, and the numerous curtain-calls presaged a hit, a palpable hit. Lerner rushed backstage to Harrison's dressing-room, meeting Marlene Dietrich on the way "who was all in white from top to toe, her face covered in white powder." She embraced him so forcefully that when they separated, her face looked bared in one spot while his acquired a powdery patch.

The reviews were confirmation of an extraordinary hit. John Chapman proclaimed that "Everything about 'My Fair Lady' is distinctive and distinguished." Robert Coleman called it a glittering musical, "as perfect an entertainment as the most fastidious playgoer could demand." Walter Kerr urged: "Don't bother to finish reading this review now. You'd better sit right down and send for those tickets to 'My Fair Lady.'" "It's Fetching-Well Done!" applauded the headline in the *Journal-American*. William Hawkins called the opening "a legendary evening," and Brooks Atkinson heartily approved of turning Shaw into a revel, though the critic drew Rex Harrison's wrath for not giving proper due to Lerner. George Jean Nathan, not one for any bandwagon, eagerly promoted the musical: "It is a fine, handsome, melodious, witty, and beautifully acted show," adjudging it the best of the season. In a lighter vein, two months later, he honoured Harrison, Andrews, Hart, Beaton, Smith, Loewe, and Lerner with his own award — chocolate "Georgies," "the only edible and hence most desirable of all the various prizes for conspicuous theatrical achievement." Irving Berlin wired Moss Hart: "You've made it awfully difficult for anyone writing a musical this season."

There were some objections, to be sure. Nathan thought that Harrison sang badly and danced like Casey Stengel. Wolcott Gibbs felt something had been lost by the romanticism — especially in the characterization of Alfred P. Doolittle who became "a healthier and much less complicated scoundrel than he was in the original." *Variety* moaned that "despite the gaiety and infectiousness of the Loewe score, there isn't a real audience-stampeding song in the show." And Eric Bentley, who always could be counted upon to sound pedantically earnest, castigated the show for being "un-Shavian in spirit" because it cancelled out "most of the points that are made in *Pygmalion.*" He argued: "Mr. Shaw's play, like all Mr. Shaw's plays, begins in parody of romance and melodrama. The people who make films and shows out of Mr. Shaw's plays go back to a point before the beginning. They return to that very romance and melodrama which Mr. Shaw spent all his energies getting away from. Certainly he is their friend in that his prose raises the level of their entertainment whenever they quote it without change. But they shouldn't ask to be regarded as his friends as their whole effort is to undo what he spent the best part of a century doing." But even the purist in Bentley could not deny that the show had its own charms; however, in recommending that audiences attend it, he added that they should leave in the interval to return home and read the last act of *Pygmalion!*

Naturally, Lerner and Loewe speculated about what Shaw would say if he ever saw *My Fair Lady*. They hoped that he would be pleased, though Lerner confessed in the Broadway *Playbill*: "I should hate to think that I might also have to contend with an irate Shaw standing at the gate [of eternity] waiting for me too." Perhaps, but the Old Boy could certainly take some pride in the fact that his name and text had added many cubits to Broadway's stature.

Beyond Broadway

ON THE SUNDAY AFTER THE OPENING, the cast assembled at 10 a.m. in a large Columbia recording studio — a converted Gothic church at 207 East 30th Street — to record the score under the supervision of Goddard Lieberson. A composer in his own right and a personal friend of Lerner and Loewe, he had been instrumental in obtaining the financial backing for *My Fair Lady* and had become what Lerner calls "the unchallenged specialist in translating theatrical scores to disc." He insisted that only the show's tunes should be recorded and none of the dialogue, so as not to bore anybody who had not seen the play. There was a technical problem with this, however, because the climax of the show was in a line of dialogue by Higgins. Lieberson decided to go directly from "I've Grown Accustomed to Her Face" into "a dramatic and emotional orchestral reprise of 'I Could Have Danced All Night' — Eliza's theme — which then built to a climax."

The session started with Stanley Holloway performing "With a Little Bit o' Luck," for which Lerner had to change a line. In order not to offend anyone with an overly delicate sensitivity to Doolittle's use of the Lord's name, Lerner, according to Lees, altered "for God's sake get me to the church on time" to "be sure and get me . . ." This did not diminish the song's earthy humour or spontaneous exhilaration. Further mirth was had with the outburst of "The Rain in Spain," where Lieberson had Harrison, Coote, and Andrews perform it before the microphones exactly as choreographed in the theatre.

By Lees' account, Franz Allers claimed that the recording was completed only at 3 a.m. on Monday but Lerner stated that it ended shortly after midnight — perhaps because he found the work far less taxing than did the performers.

The album jacket had already been prepared two weeks earlier. It was an Al Hirschfeld cartoon that showed George Bernard Shaw as a master-puppeteer pulling the strings of Rex Harrison and Julie Andrews. After Lerner had heard the complete recording, he phoned Lieberson to thank him: "Goddard, it's terrific. If it sells 50,000 albums I'll be satisfied." Little was he prepared for the phenomenon that followed. Within three months of the New York opening, the album sales had gone wild. With word of a forthcoming London production, the English were all too eager to buy the recording in advance. Lerner discovered that "the black market sale of the American cast album became a flourishing industry in England. Stewards on ocean liners and airplanes were smuggling them in by the thousands and selling them at twice and three times the original cost." In the first year of its release, the album sold 1,000,000 copies and made a substantial profit.

The show itself played to packed houses, with Standing Room Only at every performance. It won the New York Drama Critics Circle Award in an unparalleled unanimous vote, and at the 1957 Tony Awards it easily equalled the record for the most Tony's for a musical, set earlier by *South Pacific* and *Damn Yankees*, winning nine — among which were Best Actor, Best Director, Best Musical, Best Author, Best Producer, Best Composer, Best Conductor/Musical Director, Best Scenic Designer, and Best Costume Designer. Unfortunately, Julie Andrews lost as Best Actress to Judy Holiday (*Bells Are Ringing*), and Stanley Holloway (who remains the best musical Doolittle in memory) found himself pitted against fellow cast-member Robert Coote and thereby on the losing side against Sydney Chaplin (*Bells Are Ringing*).

The Mark Hellinger Theatre accommodated forty standees. For the next three years, line-ups at the box-office began at midnight, when anxious ticket-buyers equipped themselves with sleeping bags, blankets, and food in preparation for the 9:30 a.m. seat-sale. Lerner was enormously relieved: "I had, at long last, written something that I truly liked and, by glorious coincidence, so did the audience." As Rex Harrison recalled: "All the great and the good, the rich and the famous and the talented, presidents and kings came to see the show, and congratulate one or other of us afterwards . . ." The show became a cult for some — not the least of whom was Cole Porter, whose great enthusiasm for the words and music, impelled him to see the show every week.

Accolades poured in from many, but the cast was particularly flattered to win plaudits from performers of the stature of Spencer Tracy, Frank Sinatra, and Louis Armstrong. Harrison was particularly thrilled to be told by the great "Satchmo" that he had perfect pitch and that he had "hit the note right down the middle every time!"

Harrison played his role until November of the following year, when he handed over the part to Edward Mulhare. Julie Andrews stayed with the show until the London production required her, handing over her Broadway assignment to Sally Ann Howes. Holloway and Coote were succeeded by Ronald Radd and Reginald Denny respectively. *My Fair Lady* sold out throughout its first two years on Broadway, even as an American touring production began a successful circuit, with Brian Aherne and Anne Rogers. In total, the show lasted six years and nine months in the United States.

This was all fine and dandy in America, but the British must have been piqued at the cheek of having had their Shaw so appropriated. Actually, though, they suffered more from envious yearning, and it was very gratifying to them once plans were unveiled for a London production, scheduled to open 30 April 1958 at Drury Lane Theatre under the aegis of H.M. Tennent Limited. Kitty Carlisle reported that the British felt that "it was Shaw and Eliza Doolittle coming home." The advance excitement was unprecedented. One newspaper ran a daily countdown in its headlines: "Five more days . . . Four more days . . ." Ardent theatre-goers flew into London from the U.S. and other parts of Europe, and the official opening looked, according to Lerner, "more like a Coronation than a première." The audience (attired in white ties, dinner jackets, and formal gowns) accorded the musical a four-minute standing ovation and eight curtain-calls. There would have been more, but the conductor broke into "God Save the Queen."

Three nights later came a Royal Command Performance, attended by the Queen and Prince Philip, both of whom expressed delight, though the Queen remained regal and sedate during the show itself. "Don't let that disturb you," an English Member of Parliament said to Lerner. "After all, she's more German than English."

The English reviewers were as charmed as their American counterparts. The *Theatre World Annual (London)* declared in its pictorial review: "One can only hazard a guess as to what the unpredictable Shaw might have thought of this musical adaptation of his play, but one is fairly confident in affirming that the strictest purist would fall under the spell of *My Fair Lady*, without doubt astonished at the show's elegant charm, tastefulness and sincerity. He might even have a sneaking suspicion that these Americans — aided by a splendid team of English actors and actresses — have improved on the great master, triumphantly overcoming the hysterical publicity launched ahead of the London production." Trying not to be a knee-jerk chorus to her hosanna-singing colleagues, Caryl Brahms found herself undeniably enchanted by Andrews's movements and air, Harrison's "preposterously professional charm and personality — his precision of timing and technique," and the music. "Never have numbers been more skilfully used to light up and lift a scene, so that the old text, like spring, comes round again, and flowers, like the prunus, in the most natural, disarming and refreshing way."

The only note of disapproval came from a *French* newspaper critic, and even the normally acerbic Kenneth Tynan became a fan: " 'Was all the hysteria justified?' one read on Thursday morning, *à propos* of the uproar at Drury Lane last Wednesday night. The nerve of the question took one's breath away, coming as it did from the very journalists who had created the hysteria. Those who beat drums are in no position to complain of being deafened. Let us forget about the hysteria associated with *My Fair Lady* and point instead to the rare, serene pleasure it communicates, a pleasure arising from the fact that it treats both the audience and *Pygmalion* with civilized respect." Tynan complimented the show for not bullying with noise or "irrelevant displays of physical agility," and for maintaining an "intimate, light, and lyrical" tone throughout. Praising everything from Oliver Smith's lovely décor and Cecil Beaton's "dashing dresses," to musical director Robert Russell Bennett's creative arrangements, Tynan lavished special praise on Lerner and Loewe: "They have drawn song out of Shaw's people, not imposed it on them. Mr Lerner's words are wily enough for Gilbert, and Mr Loewe's contribution . . . is a tapestry of interwoven themes, crisscrossing and unexpectedly recurring . . . ." But Tynan was shrewd to perceive that "for all its grace and buoyancy, what holds the show together at the last is its determination to put character first." Turning his attention to the actors, he found Holloway to be "the fruitiest of Doolittles," Coote "the most subtly pompous of Pickerings," Andrews "a first-rate Eliza" ("once she has shed her fraudulent accent"), and Harrison an "effortless" Higgins.

The London production had a new Mrs. Higgins in Zena Dare, and, in some ways, a new Julie Andrews and Rex Harrison, for Andrews had had to brush up on her Cockney and restore the heavy accent she had toned down for Broadway, while Harrison now pitched his role directly to his compatriots, increasing his speed and using more rhetorical technique than he had in America.

Some of these differences are sensed in the London cast-recording, for the musical direction is far more rushed, and Harrison sounds less suave than fussy. His reading is more pointed, and, as Kurt Gänzl notes, "more obvious, perforated with odd growling noises and, notably, a little more sung where previously it had been spoken." Some felt that Harrison's London performance was a deterioration in standards. Lees says that in New York, Moss Hart had cautioned the star: "We have a cast full of comedians and we have a cast full of singers. . . . You are the acerbic edge of this show." In London, however, Harrison lost much of this edge in his diligence to be suavely charming in much the manner of his customary drawing-room comedy parts. The London cast album captures this, and Miles Kreuger claims: "If you compare the original 1956 Broadway cast album with the 1958 London cast album with the 1964 movie soundtrack, you hear the performance of Rex Harrison growing blunter and less sharp and immensely less adequate. He is the only major actor I have ever heard of who grew progressively incompetent in a major leading role, for which he was world-famous." Nevertheless, Harrison's flaws did not harm sales for the recording which was made in both mono and stereo formats — unlike the Broadway version which, lacking the advantage of technological advancement at the time, was recorded only in mono.

As for the Theatre Royal, Drury Lane, business boomed. Every member of the Royal Family saw the show, some several times, and foreign royalty also rushed to it. Harrison and Andrews stayed with the show until 1959, when they were succeeded by Alec Clunes and Anne Rogers. A U.K. road company began in October, 1963, and lasted six months.

It was inevitable that a Hollywood film would follow, though it was not inevitable that all the original cast would repeat their roles. Warner Brothers bought the film rights for a record-breaking $5.5 million in 1964, and hired George Cukor to direct a lavish technicolour version, starring Harrison and Holloway, but substituting Wilfrid Hyde-Whyte for Robert Coote, Gladys Cooper for Cathleen Nesbitt, and Mona Washbourne for Philippa Bevans. Poor Julie Andrews, not considered sufficient box-office in film, lost her part to Audrey Hepburn who, in turn, found her singing dubbed by Marni Nixon. Actually, even Rex Harrison nearly lost his chance to film Higgins. Jack Warner wanted James Cagney to play Doolittle and Cary Grant to try Higgins. Fortunately, this idea did not go far, for when Grant was offered the role by Cukor, he replied: "Not only will I not play Higgins, if you don't put Rex Harrison in it, I won't go and see it," Harrison recalls.

According to Gene Lees, Lerner disliked the film version. He commented to Tony Thomas: "It should have been a perfect film. But again it started off on the wrong foot by not being shot in England. And to me that deprived it of its ultimate glory." True, the film has its flaws — not the least of which is an artificial studio set for Ascot, with lattice work and arches that look like lace, Ascot ladies who look like Beverly Hills models pretending to be instinctively stylish with their Forzane slouches. There is also a clumsy fantasy sequence for "Just You Wait," in which Hepburn is pertly sweet. Wilfrid Hyde-White's Pickering is a fuddy-duddy dodderer, and Hepburn is better as the radiant Cinderella at the Ball than as the Cockney flower-girl.

But there is no denying the merits of Cukor's film. Cecil Beaton's costume design is far more lavish than it had been on stage. His film Ascot is not restricted to blacks, greys, and whites, and Audrey Hepburn's dress for the tea is extravagant — slightly comic in an overpoweringly *chic* finery of white lace with accentuating black stripes, and an enormous plumed hat that along with her parasol work effectively to point up the comic content of the scene. Her Embassy Ball dress glistens, Beaton said, "like ice on trees in Switzerland," and her new coiffure is startling in its stylish mass and contour. Gladys Cooper's Mrs. Higgins is the very essence of an aesthetic intellectual — a Fabian with couturier style, rather than a conventional dowager. From a costume point of view, the story becomes (in Beaton's own words) a play about three women — Eliza, Mrs. Higgins, and Mrs. Eynsford-Hill, who are surrounded by people "all dressed as important characters." There are virtually no "extras," and, "with the exception of the tails at the Ball, and the grey frock-coats at Ascot," there are no 'repeats.' Even the Cockney characters are created as individuals, whose prototypes are to be found in "Phil May, Belcher or photographs of the period." Among the hundreds of women at the Ball and at Ascot, there is not one costume that has not been "specially designed, or re-created from museum sources, with the care and attention given to a principal's clothes."

The sets and their decoration are prodigious in detail, and the cinematography is romantic in colour. Exteriors are as romanticized as interiors, though with monochromatic restraint. The Covent Garden set, made of solid wood and plaster, is the biggest that Jack Warner built since early Errol Flynn days. Large and soaring, it looks like "a pewter-coloured Gustav Doré of London come to life." The flower women and odd market types have real authenticity, and when the artificial studio rain falls, you feel as if you are in London. Mrs. Higgins's house looks like "a Kate Greenaway-Walter Crane version of *art nouveau*," whereas Higgins's Wimpole Street residence is an intricate and ingenious arrangement with three floors and their staircases all solid for the hard professor, and with Pre-Raphaelite trophies, choice Edwardiana for the panelled library, and wallpaper authentically reproduced from unusual 1910 designs.

From opening credits to Hermes Pan's choreography to André Previn's orchestration and the acting, Cukor's film achieves a colourful sense of rhythm and romance. The overture and titles are set to a long panning shot of flowers in baskets gradually melting into vivid patterns of ladies' cloaks as guests leave the foyer of the opera-house. All the repartée in Covent Garden is perfectly orchestrated for Higgins's first song, and although Audrey Hepburn is not vulgar enough for Eliza's "squashed cabbage leaf" mode, she blossoms into an exotic creature at Ascot. Stanley Holloway does not strike a single false note as Alfred P., and Gladys Cooper is simply the most refined and glamorous Mrs. Higgins seen to date, though we miss a mother's love for her son. (Actually, I have seen only one actress capture this underlying quality — Jennifer Phipps in the 1992 Shaw Festival production of *Pygmalion*, directed by Christopher Newton.) As for Rex Harrison, he makes even simple lines sound majestically eloquent, and with his slit eyes, angular slouch, and dazzling speaking tempo, he is incomparable in his symphony of high comic arias and dramatic peaks.

When the Oscars were handed out on 5 April 1965, *My Fair Lady* won in the categories of Best Picture, Best Actor, Best Director, Best Color Cinematography (Harry Stradling), Best Art Direction (Gene Allen, Cecil Beaton, George James Hopkins), Best Sound, Best Adapted Score (André Previn), and Best Costume Design (Color) (Cecil Beaton). The only sour note was that Audrey Hepburn had not been nominated, though even if she had been, she would in all likelihood have lost to the sentimental favourite, Julie Andrews, who was compensated for playing Mary Poppins instead of Eliza Doolittle. As it happened, Hepburn graciously presented the Best Actor award to Rex Harrison who, as Julie Andrews applauded dutifully, delivered a most diplomatic tribute to his two Elizas: "Deep love to — uh — well, two fair ladies."

One measure of a musical's greatness is the number of revivals and foreign-language versions it engenders. *My Fair Lady* has splendidly withstood the test of time, with an older, more restrained Harrison reprising his great role in a 1980 production, and with such reputable stage actors as Ian Richardson and John Neville essaying Higgins on Broadway (1976) and in Stratford, Ontario (1988), respectively. *My Fair Lady* has proved itself to be one of the most popular musicals on foreign-language stages. There have been productions all over Europe and North and South America, and some in the Middle East. To add eccentricity to the legend, there have also been exotic recordings in French, German, Spanish, and Swedish, with some strange interpretations of the key roles. For example, the Elizas have ranged from the sub-operatic to the caterwauling; the Doo-littles have been heavily Jewish on occasion or in a low comic vein; and Higgins has been classily masculine or tiresomely aggressive.

Yet nothing diminishes the lustre of the musical. Indeed, it is probably fair to say that it has altered forever an audience's expecta-tions of *Pygmalion*, for how many of us can any longer sit through a performance of Shaw's sparkling comedy without hearing in our inner ears the sounds of Lerner and Loewe's lyrics and music? Do we not expect the Higgins to break into a patter-song? Do we not expect the Eliza to express her feelings in music? Do we not hope that Alfred P. will do a little jig or soft-shoe as he expounds his pragmatic philosophy? And do we not wish for a climactic finale — perhaps a strong set of strings to come from under the text and contradict the anti-romantic Shavian ending?

Alan Jay Lerner always believed that as far as his musical was concerned, "the right people at the right moment in their lives embarked on the right venture — authors, director, costumer, scenic designer, producer, lighting man, choreographer and actors — and rather than extending their talents to the limit, expressed them to the limit." But why was *My Fair Lady* such a hit and an instant legend? Why did the songs — good as they were — enjoy such unprece-dented popularity all over the world where the show became known? Why did the cast album make multi-million dollar profits for CBS's $400,000 investment? Why did the show in all its various manifes-tations gross almost $100 million?

Lerner himself was baffled, yet whenever contracts were drawn with foreign producers, he insisted that every production be an identical copy of the original Broadway production. "Who knows?" he remarked to Herman Levin. "It may have been the chandeliers that did it."

Structure, Words, and Music

LERNER AND LOEWE'S MEGA-HIT ran on Broadway for 2,717 performances, enjoyed a spectacular run in London as well (2,281 performances), and became internationally popular, with companies in Australia, Sweden, Mexico, Norway, Denmark, Finland, Holland, Russia, and Israel. It made Shaw a household word in households which had never been on reading terms with *Pygmalion*, and it made Broadway history by several elements that broke with tradition. Indeed, this departure from Broadway tradition may have accounted for some unusual minority disapproval of *My Fair Lady*'s score. *Variety* reported that composer Rudolf Friml had walked out of a performance in London, grumbling that the score was not of the type he would call music. Some musicians disliked Rex Harrison's spoken-singing, though, as Abe Laufe points out in *Broadway's Greatest Musicals* (1970), they acknowledged that nobody did it better.

Why all the astounding success for a musical that has many ingredients of classic operetta and which, today, hardly seems as daringly innovative as *Cabaret* (1966), *Sweeney Todd* (1979), or *Kiss of the Spider Woman* (1992)? The truth of the matter is that *My Fair Lady* is more subtle than at first meets the eye and ear. On the surface, it is a variation of classic operetta — with a soprano, high baritone/ tenor juveniles, a low comedian and patter man, a comic sub-plot, and a romantic story. Yet, the musical departs from the musicals of earlier eras, for as Kurt Gänzl has noted, "There are no concerted finales, no opening chorus nor any genuine ensemble of solo voices," and, in fact, Lerner and Loewe abandon the musical format of the 1950s by not having a single duet and very little ensemble work (except for "allowing the chorus to back some of the solo work").

All the major reviews (and for those who like to keep score on this

99

matter, there were seven raves and not a single pan) referred to the perfect fusion of script and libretto. John Chapman, writing in Steven Suskin's 1990 book *Opening Night on Broadway*, asserted that Lerner and Loewe wrote "much the way Shaw must have done had he been a musician instead of a music critic." Robert Coleman added that the show kept "the essence of the original," as its lyrics beautifully complemented the Shavian dialogue. "The Lerner-Loewe songs are not only delightful, they advance the action as well. They are ever so much more than interpolations, or interruptions. They are a most important and integrated element in about as perfect an entertainment as the most fastidious playgoer could demand."

In many ways, *My Fair Lady* defies the norms of romantic musicals. The outer signs of romance are subtle rather than overt: the word "love" is never mentioned by any principal character — not even the lovelorn Freddy Eynsford-Hill, who is given the only wholly explicit love-song, which, by the way, is arguably out of place in the work. As Lehman Engel observes, "there is the merest suggestion of a subplot: Alfred P. Doolittle, his beginnings, rise, and malcontent with success, but this is by no means a complete one. What is special and remarkable in this play, as in *Romeo and Juliet*, is the importance and singularity and fullness of every character. All of them revolve about Eliza *and* Higgins: the housekeeper Mrs. Pearce, Higgins's mother, Colonel Pickering, A.P. Doolittle, Freddie, and even the only once seen Hungarian Professor Karpathy, to whom is given the all-important spot of providing a period for the end of Act One in the musical." The same critic goes on to argue that the characters collectively replace the need for a subplot:

In terms of mechanics alone, Higgins and Pickering together relieve the need of Eliza's constant presence. Either man with the housekeeper, relieves the other. Mrs. Higgins with Eliza excuses Higgins. Doolittle with Eliza and/or his pals gets rid of Higgins and Pickering. Freddie's olio gives everyone else a breather. All of the players are important enough so that the combination of any two or three in a scene serves the stage's needs amply.

This is unique. If you tried to do *Oklahoma!*, for example, minus the subplot (Ado, Will and the Peddler) the remainder (Laurey, Curly, Judd, and thin old Aunt Eller) would not work. There would be too little substance and no relief for audience or performers.

In all three crucial parts of its structure — beginning, middle, end — *My Fair Lady* is extraordinarily precise, pointed, and peerless. The opening is more than simply traditional. It introduces the main themes and characters, excites an air of comedy and drama, defines a place, period, and style, and does all these things without actually predicting the show as a whole. The opening is also without music, though there is an overture and some underscoring, but there is no opening number. The street buskers serve for the Cockney ambience. Hanya Holm's choreography is selective and light. Act I contains the Ascot Gavotte, Doolittle's comic street hoofing, the Embassy Waltz (suggesting Strauss and Lehar), and, best of all, a climactic tango, where the two principals forget their respective foibles and differences in an ecstasy of celebration.

The first act manages a difficult balance. It remains true to Shavian satire while developing a romanticism that is intrinsically foreign to Shaw's express purpose. The Cockney comedy, so deftly presented in some of Eliza's songs, in enriched by Doolittle's first number that has a pub vulgarity combined with the dustman's roguish charm. Thrown out of a pub and in need of a handout for "liquid protection" against a nagging mistress, Doolittle, in the consoling company of three other loafers, runs into Eliza who gives him his song cue. She flips him a coin and proclaims: "Well, I had a bit of luck meself tonight." The word "luck" sets him off in jubilant smugness, and into a jogging, heel-and-toe dance with his three companions, in which he pronounces his philosophy of living by his wits and exploiting his vices (sloth, drunkenness, selfishness, philandering) at the expense of society. Lerner and Loewe craftily combine choral singing, Doolittle's rousing festivity, and a march tempo. The horns, brass, strings, and drums carry the celebration to a pitch of quasi-revivalist fervour.

What a startlingly vivid contrast is provided later in the act by the rigidly stylized "Ascot Gavotte," where the facial immobility, stilted posture, and coolly formal slouches of the lords and ladies satirize English reticence. Their extravagant parade, stony silence and reserve, their studied boredom and stately elegance all incarnate the art of contrivance and façade. They, and not the horses or jockeys, are very much the true spectacle. Astutely aware that the joke should not pall by protracted repetition, Lerner and Loewe contrast their utter lack of emotion at the race-track with Eliza's intractable excitement. While the elaborately-dressed crowd watches the race, without so much as a fluttering eyelash or a dilated nostril, Eliza cannot control herself as her betting favourite, Dover, trails the leaders. She urges her horse on and climactically yells out a Cockney vulgarity that shocks everyone on stage as the lights black out. (In George Cukor's film version, the conclusion is far more elaborate as the camera captures a *haute couture* set of exits while the soundtrack breaks into pure melody.)

Most of the songs in Act I fall to Eliza and Higgins (about which more in due course), and the act ends with the Embassy Waltz after Freddy's lushly amorous "On the Street Where You Live." A practical reason for this solo is to provide a necessary lapse of time for Eliza and Higgins to change into their resplendent costumes for the Embassy Ball. But there is no denying the fact that the song generates uncomfortable questions about Freddy's character and his worthiness as a foil to Higgins. A forlorn, would-be lover, he lingers around Wimpole Street, hoping to be allowed in to see Eliza, or, if not, then at least have a nosegay presented to her through the office of Mrs. Pearce. Part of his lyric is pure romance; part stamps him as the butt of comedy — a poor serenading fool, quite overpowered by feeling. His song, placed soon after the Ascot débacle, recaps the preceding scene and announces who he is. It is a tribute to the Eliza who does not know about his absolute devotion to her, and its surcharged feeling seems right out of a fairy tale or courtly myth. Freddy is the suitor put to trying labour in order to woo his beloved who, as yet, is unattainable — a *princesse lointaine*, as it were, who, all the same, might (he hopes) magically appear and incarnate his fantasy. Appropriately, his song has a soaring quality, but is it suited to the general tone and tenor of the libretto? Lehman Engel thinks not, because there is no palpable context for the song and the singer is simply "stupid." Engel likens the song to a picture that has "shoved its way out of the frame with a bang." It is, in other words, "a 'pop' song" that has "strayed into a score otherwise brilliant, integrated, with a great sense of the play's own style and a faithful, uncompromising exposition of characters and situations."

For its middle, the show dares to compress the passage of time into a sequence of drill scenes in which Eliza is put through tortuous phases of elocution lessons so that she might be successfully passed off as a duchess at the Embassy Ball. "While there are certainly no rules governing this," Lehman Engel writes, "large lapses of time seem to belong more often to plays and operas rather than to musicals." But Lerner and Loewe skilfully open up the play without losing any of Shaw's reformulated myth of metamorphosis. The drilling sequence is crystallized in a choral song by Mrs. Pearce and the entire retinue of servants, and the satiric tone is shared by all, even by Eliza, the butt of comedy, and by Higgins, the hallowed martyr (in his servants' eyes) to her cause of transformation.

The middle section is really still part of Act 1 which, as expected, is lively, entertaining, and comic without in any sense diminishing either Shaw's or Lerner and Loewe's interpretation of a creation myth. Joseph P. Swain has written that unlike its predecessors (such as Rodgers and Hart's *A Connecticut Yankee* (1927), Cole Porter's *Out of This World* (1950), or Jerome Moross-John Latouche's *The Golden Apple* (1953), *My Fair Lady* translates "deeper mythic elements into dramatic terms" — specifically the element of Pygmalion's initial misogyny. Indeed, Lerner and Loewe carry Shaw's Pygmalion myth to a radically interesting closure. Their Higgins, while dressed in Pygmalion's misogyny, establishes his own character "in a way that begins to interpret the myth."

The first act devotes three songs to Higgins — two of which could be generally classified as solos (with some choral cueing) — and four to Eliza — three of which are essentially solos. The slight edge that Eliza has in number of songs is probably caused by the fact that she is the title-character who causes essential change in her antagonist as well as in herself. A simpler reason could be the fact that the role calls for a soprano voice that complements Freddy's tenor and offsets the patter and/or vaudevillian character of Higgins's and Doolittle's songs. Moreover, true to Shaw's dialectic, the songs of Higgins and Eliza crystallize the linguistic, social, and psychological conflicts between the professor-autocrat and his naïve but vital pupil.

Higgins's songs are the most emphatic, pointed expressions in lyric form of the character's unshakeable belief in the authority and majesty of the English language and in his own role as a proselytizing monarch of rhetoric. Of course, allied to his notion of linguistic supremacy is that of gender imperialism. He is as assured of his own unimpeachable rank as master-dialectician as he is resolved to be immunized against women and their romantic sentimentality, which he considers a contemptible weakness. His opening number, "Why Can't the English?" is the first piece of the musical that combines words and music, and it is placed in Covent Garden — after his intimidating eavesdropping on Eliza and her fellow Cockneys. Questioned about his identity, he demonstrates his phonetical expertise in dialogue exchanges before breaking into song, whose theme is "the divine gift of articulate speech" — the very sort of power that issues from "Shakespeare and Milton and the Bible" and that lifts a human above the sordidness and wretchedness of slum-life. As in all his numbers, Higgins enunciates exquisitely and expands his thesis in formally intricate verse that transcends the superficial virtuosity and playfulness of the average patter-song — the type found so abundantly in Gilbert and Sullivan, for example. Higgins's thesis on the relationship between language and social/cultural rank informs the whole song, though this nucleus is embedded in long lines of quantitative verse, while the supporting plasm is wittily shaped and marked by throwaway epigrams, as in: "In France every Frenchman knows his language from 'A' to 'Zed' / The French never care what they do, actually, as long as they pronounce it properly." As is proper to his professional background, Higgins shows himself to be a master of rhyming diction, delighting in slant rhymes and in phrases that employ caesura and enjambment with equal finesse.

His loquacity, quick turns of phrase, supercilious wit, and command of rhyme and metre interact with his scorn for linguistic and social vulgarians who lack his passion for language. This song is not meant to be a clap-trap show-stopper, but a vehicle for establishing his personality and for dramatizing several of Shaw's themes. One of the most clever touches is Lerner's use of other characters to interrupt or cue Higgins. For example, Eliza's shrieks and wails prompt his mocking imitation, as well as a brief interplay with Pickering in order to underscore theme and complete a rhyme pattern:

HIGGINS

>Chickens cackling in a barn . . .
>(Pointing to ELIZA)
>Just like this one —!

ELIZA

>— Garn!

HIGGINS

>I ask you, sir, what sort of word is that?
>It's 'Aooow' and 'Garn' that keep her in her place.
>Not her wretched clothes and dirty face.

This type of intersection, delay, and resumption makes for a very dynamic and creative sequence, where Higgins can stop and start the melody, pause for a little patter on the side, and launch into full-blown *sprechstimme*, all the while consolidating the impression of his arrogant, manipulative personality.

In contrast, Eliza's first number, prompted by a couple of florins dropped by Higgins into her flower-basket, is lyrical in a wholly Cockney mode — a point pictorially realized by the setting, and one rhetorically manifested by her diction and theme. Her assonantal wail "Aaah-ow-ooh!" that grows progressively longer in the repetition becomes a refrain in the song to mark her pleased astonishment and mock-haughtiness before setting her off on her daydream of creature comforts. The supporting quartet of males provides a barbershop accompaniment, but she is the vocal and imagistic centre, the maiden yearning not just for a "room somewhere," with an "enormous chair," a coal fire, and "lots of chocolate," but for someone "warm and tender" as well who will take "good care" of her. The Cockney talent for new-coined compounds is shown in her word "absobloominlutely" that pairs off with the "Aaah-owooh" to stamp her distinctive sounds and fantasticating ability on our minds.

"Wouldn't It Be Loverly?" (with its moderate tempo) reveals her character in sharp contrast to Higgins's. She fantasizes optimistically rather than cynically or satirically. The music here, according to Swain, is composed "in a light Broadway texture, but its phrasing lends an impression of sincerity quite absent in Higgins's music." The melodic climax makes her wistfulness credible and poignant.

Eliza is passionate in her songs, illustrating shifts of mood more dramatically than Higgins does through most of the first act. In "Just You Wait," after Higgins has bombarded her with vowel sounds, insisting that she practise relentlessly, she is tormented into a rage. But this anger takes a comic form because her fantasy of revenge is exaggeratedly self-promoting and gloriously vernacular. The Cockney accent gives it extra colour and passion, and the pronounced assonance is true to her untutored character and visceral reactions: "Ooooooooo 'enry 'iggins! / Just you wait until we're swimmin' in the sea! / Ooooooooo 'enry 'iggins! / And you get a cramp a little ways from me!" The song is actually in two parts, with the first being brisk and hot-tempered, and the second, beginning with "One day I'll be famous! I'll be proper and prim," growing balladic in its demands on vocal register before returning to the full measure and cadence of comic Cockney wish-fulfilment: " 'Thanks a lot, King,' says I, in a manner well-bred; / 'But all I want is 'enry 'iggins 'ead!' "

Her next solo is "I Could Have Danced All Night," which she sings after having been wafted on a cloud of exultation. Having successfully dropped her old accent and learned Higgins's models of diction and elocution, she breaks into lush romanticism. Although the servants afford a counterpointing staccato and alternative rhyme, she is a soloist here, a bird that has finally spread its wings. The question is whether she is celebrating Higgins's "interest" in her and, so, missing the point of his experiment. But her sheer joyous abandon makes us put aside the question for a moment.

Henry Higgins stands in total contrast to Eliza, though it is his songs that really begin to interpret the Pygmalion myth. His second solo ("I'm an Ordinary Man") has a two-part structure: in the first, Higgins describes himself; in the second, he describes the nefarious effects a woman would have upon him. This solo, with its spoken introduction, grows directly out of a context. After Pickering declares that Eliza is not to be taken advantage of, and asks his colleague if he is "a man of good character where women are concerned," Higgins dramatically asserts the bad effects of women upon men. Consisting of three eleven-line verses, six seven-liners, and two four-line interludes — a total of eighty-three lines — the song is a brilliant set-piece of dramatically shifting registers and tones that require an actor-singer of mercurially quick tempi and modulations. Higgins claims to be "an ordinary man" of "no eccentric whim," who is "free of strife," until a woman interferes with his serenity. The *moderato* opening has a gently measured amiability that amuses by its exaggeration. The self-idealization is warped. The second section begins a dramatic change in tone, melody, and tempo, as Higgins drops his placid composure to sound notes of turbulent gender conflicts and abrupt rage. Here the *allegro molto vivo* establishes his misogyny by periodic phrasing and brassy orchestration. A transitional pattern is repeated, so that the passages of sweetness alternate with those of stormy irascibility, until with the cresting passion and tempo, Higgins becomes increasingly onomatopoeic, rapidly piling up images of loud discord. He develops a mimetic pitch on "She'll have a large Wagnerian mother / With a voice that shatters glass!" so that his voice takes on a shattering quality, and then he turns on all the studio machines at full volume, resulting in cacophony. The song ends with a single statement of unflinching bravado: "I shall never let a woman in my life!"

Joseph P. Swain has articulated the subtleties of the musical composition, indicating that the "quick dotted rhythms" of the first section "trip along more in the manner of the lightest intermezzo than of a soliloquy," thereby yielding an interesting nuance. Higgins does not appear to be what he claims to be. The second section, with its increased tempo, wood winds, horn, trumpet, and xylophone accompaniment, has a "vaudevillian superficiality." It is comic without being quite real, and, so, is "the first hint of Loewe's reinterpretation of the Pygmalion myth: if Higgins' self-image must be questioned, then so must his misogyny." And if we buy into Loewe's version, then we are prepared accordingly for the closure of the romantic gap in Shaw's original ending.

Lerner's Pygmalion begins his creation of a Galatea with the drilling sequence already mentioned above. The only emotion he shows at first relates directly to language, but he does make one concession to abandon, and this comes in "The Rain in Spain" number that has the very stuff of whole-hearted improvisation. The placement of the song is splendidly effective, coming as it does after the chorus of servants who sympathize with Higgins rather than Eliza. With Eliza's sudden, unexpected grace of pronunciation, Higgins bursts into a triumphant cry ("By George, she's got it!") — and there is a choral structure quickly established by Higgins, Eliza, and Pickering, who are all simultaneously caught up in the same uninhibited celebration. Eliza's emotional release represents her relief at success, as well as an assumption that she is now a partner with Higgins in his experiment. The men, on the other hand, revert to their exclusive "clubbiness" once the moment is over, and they exclude Eliza from their smug self-congratulation.

During the song itself, all serious matters are held in suspension, as Eliza's line, "The rain in Spain stays mainly in the plain!", feeds into a tango rhythm. Higgins's charade of bull-fighting with Pickering as the bull, and the clapping of hands and flamenco stamping of feet are so radically different from the very English character of the other songs as to make this moment endearingly warm and sunny. The tango, according to Swain, in the mould of a classic set-piece, heightens the emotion "far beyond the level of any speech" and "caps the joy of creation."

The final part of the musical begins with a lyrical peak, the Embassy Ball, where the dramatic suspense is generated by the question of whether the Hungarian speech expert, Professor Karpathy, will unmask Eliza as a phoney duchess. But this becomes an anti-climax, because upon the return to Wimpole Street of Higgins, Eliza, and Pickering, a most dramatic scene takes shape. Elated at Eliza's triumph, the two men sing "You Did It," supported by a chorus of servants. This brisk melody of egotistical self-congratulation enrages Eliza who feels totally slighted by their disregard for her vital contribution to their project. She returns the expensive jewellery, demands to know what clothes she may keep, and storms out of the house after a perplexed Higgins calls her "ungrateful." Here she meets the loitering Freddy and is further vexed by her suitor's apparent shyness and inability to make love to her openly and directly. Her sharp reaction to his mere words is a rebuff in song, which the hapless fellow never deflects as she storms up and down the stage in her anger at men in general. Alas, this song does more for her fresh wilfulness than for Freddy's character, but the psychological relationship of the pair is brought into intriguing focus, as we see from Freddy's impotent gestures and reactions. He is frightened, bewildered, happy, but completely overpowered, as she "crowns" him with her suitcase before marching off, and it is clear that his panting ardour and longing make him a willing devotee to a highly individualistic woman. Eliza is in control of this man — though not of Higgins. But why would she want to marry this insipid, lustreless, weak fool? An answer suggests itself: she is no mere doll, no sweet ingénue, or manipulated puppet. She is a woman in her own right who will not be taken for granted or shrugged off by any man. Unable to be an equal partner as yet with a man who is a real match (in wills) with her, she will subjugate Freddy, her boy-toy.

Once again departing from Broadway custom, *My Fair Lady* has a second act that deepens the serious (rather than the comic) notes of the first. Even the case of Alfred P. Doolittle advances the matter. His second set-piece, "Get Me to the Church on Time," does nothing for the main plot, but does serve two important functions. It provides a change of pace and substitutes song and dance in place of Shavian stage-philosophy. While this latter function at first seems radically at odds with the seriousness of the musical, Lerner and Loewe cleverly ensure that the roisterous energy and tone translate Doolittle's philosophy into action. After "With a Little Bit o' Luck" — a song about his belief in easy living — "Get Me to the Church on Time" celebrates Doolittle's last night of bachelor freedom in a lively production number. As Abe Laufe sums up, "To some Shavian admirers, the lyrics for both songs may not seem as pungent as Doolittle's speeches in *Pygmalion*, but to musical comedy devotees, they are far more effective as songs than they would have been as dialogue." It is a matter of the mode being perfectly attuned to the resonance and pitch of the character's philosophy.

Aside from "Show Me" and "Get Me to the Church on Time," the second act concentrates structurally, lyrically, and musically on the Eliza-Higgins relationship and, more importantly, on a form for the Pygmalion myth. It employs reprises of "Just You Wait," "On the Street Where You Live," and "Wouldn't It Be Loverly?" not because the composers need to sentimentalize old melodies and lyrics, but because there are dramatic functions for these reprises. Usually, the idea that the same lyric can apply to the first and second acts is suspect, because principal characters can be expected to change radically and, consequently, their lyrics should reflect this fact. However, the reprises in the second act of *My Fair Lady* are the musical's answer to opera's *leitmotif*, and just as many of Verdi's and Wagner's greatest musical passages depend upon a carefully developed *leitmotif* scheme, so does the music of *My Fair Lady* depend upon the braiding of dramatic contexts and themes.

The reprises in the second act help us to recall the original contexts as we experience the new ones, and this gives rise to a number of possible ironies and meanings. When Eliza revives but one verse of "Just You Wait," it is because Higgins has still not awakened to her individual genius as a newly created or recreated being with a spark of her own. In fact, a careful study of the verse reveals a subtle change in lyric, as Eliza uses words she did not use when she first sang the song: "You will be the one it's done to; / And you'll have no one to run to." This, says Swain, is Lerner and Loewe's version of what musicologists would call *contrafactum* — their version being more of the later variety that converted one sort music to another by a new set of words, rather than the older variety where a text of vocal music was replaced by an entirely new one. The crafty change in lyric exposes a new dramatic situation for Eliza, one in which she is prepared to be a feisty Galatea. Her smouldering fury is not reduced by her uncontrollable sobs after Higgins's insulting dismissal of her importance to him. Her tearful response reveals her hurt, but it has an underlying strength, for it feeds into her "Show Me" number where Freddy receives the brunt of her anger. Her next piece of music comes with her brief return to the Covent Garden Flower Market, where, "more alone than she has ever been," she reprises a verse of "Wouldn't It Be Loverly?". Once again, the point is not simply a *de rigueur* nostalgic Broadway tour of the past, but an expression of her radical change as a woman. She is unrecognized by her former cohorts who feel uncomfortable in her transformed presence. Eliza, the reprised verse makes clear, cannot really go back home again, for she is now out of place — an alien whose notion of being a lady bears a heavy price.

But it is Higgins who has the two most effective dramatic reprises. "A Hymn to Him" shows his exasperation over women, and its changing metre, polysyllabic rhyme, quick outburst of patter-wit, and final assertion of his egotism ally it to "I'm an Ordinary Man." From the "hymn," it would appear that Higgins will not change in his patronizing arrogance, chauvinistic disdain, or heartless insensitivity to Eliza. He is convinced that she is nothing significant in his life, and he needs an object lesson in humility and wisdom. Higgins ignores the point of "Without You," which Eliza sings to his face in order to teach him that the universe and she will somehow survive without him. However, he staunchly refuses to be humble. He resorts to a *contrafactum* in order to immunize himself against any assault on his apparently inviolable male pride: "By George, I really did it! / I did it! I did it! / I said I'd make a woman / And indeed I did!" This lyric revives memories of the very early morning after the Embassy Ball, when, along with Pickering, he lauded their own achievement in Eliza's fancy-dress transformation. The one crucial difference is that Higgins, for all his boastful self-glorification, is now also genuinely surprised and delighted at Eliza's magnificent new strength. It is possibly a case of two volatile chemicals requiring each other for a necessary reaction.

The true climax of the Pygmalion-Galatea myth is certainly the "I've Grown Accustomed to Her Face" number. According to Swain "The lyric is still of a pattering sort, as all the lyrics for Higgins are, but for once the language is simple, direct, and honest, as a confession should be. The music is by far the most serious of the play." The song comes on gradually, like an organic outgrowth of some vague but irresistible urge. Stung by Eliza's insistence that she can get along without him, Higgins stomps across the stage, furious that he has let a woman into his life — the very thing he deemed unconscionable in Act 1. The first rendition of the main song is followed by an interlude — a musical soliloquy, in which he imagines the consequences, at first bitterly, then with fiendish pleasure, of Eliza's "infantile," "heartless, wicked, brainless" idea of wanting to marry Freddy. Says Joseph P. Swain: "The rhythm within each phrase, a few quick notes ending with a very long note, adds to this musing quality by making each one appear to be spontaneous and independent, almost like talking to oneself, and yet the overall phrase structure is clearly designed for motion." This interlude bears some resemblance to Eliza's "Just You Wait," another fantasy song, though there are differences in the metre and rhythm. Swain raises an intriguing question: "Does this turnabout on the revenge motive imply a mutual affinity between the two protagonists, who have been portrayed so differently throughout, or merely that Higgins' emotional maturity is at a stage comparable to Eliza's at the beginning of the play?"

The fantasy has a crafty dynamic: it shifts from tranquil self-idealization to a swift, forceful vengefulness, and does so in the borrowed mode of "I'm an Ordinary Man." Now all these sly reprises are linked to one another, and all lead directly into the principal motive of the main song. The rhythm changes with Higgins's wistfulness — a perfect illustration that the stubborn professor has softened, and within a mere twenty bars, Lerner and Loewe cleverly suggest a failure of his self-assurance, a breakdown of his revenge, and a new emotion that baffles him with its hitherto unsuspected power. There is "a deft slowing of rhythm" and "a strong cadence on the down-beat. The accumulated power of this delayed cadence, Swain believes, with the lyric in the last phrase emphasizing 'her looks,' 'her voice,' 'her face,' underlines the cause of Higgins' new wonder at himself." The self-imagined misogynist has surprised himself by discovering that he loves a woman, even though he never names his feeling.

Writing in the *New Republic* on 9 April 1956, Eric Bentley objected to what he called the "utter sentimentalization" of Lerner's ending. He thought that Higgins had been turned into "the standard leading man of musical comedy and at that as cornily love-lorn as they come." In another piece, Bentley carped: "Higgins, who had been the very type of eccentric professor, becomes an average man and is celebrated as such in a song. . . . The notion that (Eliza) would marry him springs from a very cool calculation as to what the public would lick its chops over." But as Swain retorts, the ending is effective in its own terms. Higgins's relationship with Eliza is "developed with consistent subtlety — the word 'love' never comes between them — through the music of the play," and Lerner and Loewe "forswear all serious devices of romantic expression that the Broadway tradition makes available to them, so that even 'I've Grown Accustomed to Her Face,' the weightiest number of the play is restrained in overt expression." Swain goes on to call this song "the capstone of the play because it is in that moment that the mythic elements are fixed. . . . The transformation of the principal motives in the song reveals that the principal characters have reversed roles. Eliza is the sculptor, after all, and Higgins the block." Lerner himself seems to have been aware of this, for in "Shavian Musical Notes" for the *New York Times* of 11 March 1956, he wrote: "In a far less tangible way, Higgins goes through as much of a transformation as Eliza, the only difference being that Shaw would never allow the transformation to run its natural course." And although Lerner in a special note for the musical asked Shaw and Heaven to forgive him for the new ending, he suspected that he (and not Shaw) was right.

Appendix I: A BRIEF HISTORY
OF THE BROADWAY MUSICAL

ALMOST FORTY YEARS after its Broadway opening, *My Fair Lady* is still considered to be in a class by itself as musical theatre. Whether it is "The greatest musical of the twentieth century" — as Brooks Atkinson once contended in Alan Jay Lerner's *The Musical Theatre: A Celebration* — is a moot point. However, it is incontestable that its three most important elements — book, music, lyrics — have a distinction of their own, carrying the musical far beyond what Kern and Hammerstein's *Show Boat* had already achieved in 1927, or *Oklahoma!* had spectacularly gained for the genre in 1943. More than any of its predecessors, *My Fair Lady* (while adding to Broadway tradition) exploited a literary classic for a popular commercial form, without betraying its source in most of its essential nuances and textures.

It is now a well-worn truism to say, as Martin Gottfried has, that "the musical is America's most significant contribution to world theater." Although there are general antecedents in such earlier works as John Gay's *The Beggar's Opera* in the eighteenth-century or in the comic operettas of Gilbert and Sullivan in the nineteenth, musicals, as they have come to be known from the third decade of the twentieth century, are "purely American as a stage form," being outgrowths "of vaudeville's basic song and dance."

A quick overview of the history of the American musical reveals several generations of development. It is claimed that the Broadway musical started in 1866, when a visiting ballet company from Paris lost its New York booking to a theatre fire and was then hurriedly added to a melodrama called *The Black Crook* at Niblo's Garden, on the northeast corner of Broadway and Prince Street. Steven Suskin relates that this show lasted 474 performances, thriving on its alluring *danseuses* in pink-coloured tights. But the commercial Broadway theatre, as we know it, began to develop in the late 1880s, and owed most explicit debts to Italian opera-buffa (operas with dialogue and light music). In Paris this genre was called *opéra-comique* (later *opéra-bouffe*), and the creations of Daniel Auber, Adolphe Adam, and Gaetano Donizetti gave rise to the operettas of Hervé (Florimond Ronger), Jacob Offenbach, and Johann Strauss II. These composers emphasized light melodic music that was clearly influenced by Mozart and Rossini. Offenbach's *Orfée aux Enfers* (1859), designed by the illustrious Gustav Doré, was a musical with dialogue that retold in contemporary form the story of Orpheus by Glück. The modern recasting — where Orpheus and Eurydice are a quarrelsome married couple who speak in Parisian patois, and where Orpheus plays a violin instead of a lute, and wretchedly at that — was condemned by the critics of the day but eagerly embraced by audiences. Offenbach established an operetta style that emphasized wit and dramatic characterization liberated from tragic arias and high drama. As Alan Jay Lerner notes in his highly idiosyncratic survey, *The Musical Theatre*, Offenbach was indeed "the father" of all modern composers by having works such as *La Belle Hélène* (1868) and *The Tales of Hoffman* (1881) performed in the repertoire of opera houses the world over.

Offenbach was a progenitor, in a fundamental way, of Gilbert and Sullivan, for his highly successful comic operetta *The Brigands* (1869) inspired *The Pirates of Penzance* (1879) in a way that Lerner believes "exceeds all bounds of coincidence." It was from Offenbach that the great English duo learned to exploit satire and light verse with clever rhymes. *The Mikado* (1885) was, perhaps, their greatest success, achieving a satire and comic texture by its parodic grafting of British manners to Japanese characters. Gilbert and Sullivan transformed the knockabout burlesque and Cockney music-hall turns of British society into comic operetta of enduring lyrical satire and gaiety. They stood in counterpoint to other European masters of operetta who, like Johann Strauss II and Franz Lehar, emphasized music rather than lyric, embellishing it with Viennese rhythms and tempi. Lyrics in Viennese operetta tended to be platitudinous in works even by

Emmerich Kalman (*The Countess Mariza*) (1926), Leo Fall (*The Dollar Princess*) (1909), and Oscar Straus (*A Waltz Dream*) (1908). Even Lehar's *The Merry Widow* (1907), one of the most popular musicals even in our own day, has lyrics in translation that generate mild ridicule. "Come where the leafy bowers lie" is, as Lerner cracks, "Not a lyric for a tenor with bridge-work."

The Europeans bequeathed a legacy of light classical music and comic lyrics to American composers. In the 1913–14 season, the major hits were Victor Herbert's *Sweethearts* and Rudolf Friml's *High Jinks*, both of which were operettas with a distinctly European flavour, and native American creativity was dressed in borrowed robes. Gerald Bordman contends that as long as Vienna and the rest of Europe offered superior craftsmanship and memorably melodic scores, "it was difficult for Americans to compete." The composers with the most indigenous accents were confined to writing occasional tunes for revues, though the seasons from mid-1914 to mid-1921 were "possibly the most exciting in the history of the American Musical Theatre." Disenchantment with Europe and things European mixed with American self-awareness to produce a new self-confidence. Moreover, a new American idiom called "ragtime" spread from the Midwest and the South to Broadway, and singers were adding this music to their repertoires. Jazz soon followed, and the pronounced "black" style heightened the maturing American character of musical theatre.

Not that European influence vanished. However, the American composers transformed their admiration of older European models into something paradoxically indigenous. Victor Herbert (born in Dublin, trained in Berlin) established his own American brand of "light opera" in the 1890s complemented by what Suskin calls "native songshows, filled with low-brow jokes and randomly interpolated Tin Pan Alley ditties." Herbert led the American musical in the era just preceding and continuing with World War I with popular works such as *Babes in Toyland* (1903), *Naughty Marietta* (1910), and *Eileen* (1917). The masses enjoyed the ethnic slant of the new entertainments — the Irishness of Harrigan and Hart, the "Dutch" (actually German) of Weber and Fields — which paved the way for the stereotypical characters and stories of George M. Cohan's simplistic but professionally brash musical comedy form.

Then Irving Berlin, called "America's Franz Schubert" by George Gershwin, made modern musical theatre a robust American form, before Jerome Kern, an avid Anglophile who (as Richard Rodgers noted) had one foot in Europe and the other in America, joined forces with P.G. Wodehouse, a lyricist descended from Gilbert, to bring charm, literacy, and rhyming ingenuity to the Broadway stage. "Before Noel Coward, I AM!" could have been either Kern's or Wodehouse's boast, for the pair (quickly expanded into a trio by Guy Bolton) perfected a form that was praised by the acerbic Dorothy Parker for its casual sliding of action into songs that rhymed deftly. Indeed, Parker's review of *Oh, Lady! Lady!!* (1918) was, in effect, a pithy summing-up of the Princess Theater shows — vehicles that were genuine little musical plays, elegantly adorned by star performers of the day, with large choruses of ensembles, comedic situations, integrated music and lyrics, and a neatly structured libretto.

Despite the Jazz Age, Great Crash, and Depression in the 1930s, operetta — as Lerner noted — did not suffer a violent death. Its American masters all had deeply European connections, with names such as Berlin, Kern, Gershwin, Youmans, Dietz, Schwartz, Harbach, Friml, Romberg, Rodgers, Hart, and Hammerstein all tracing lineages back to Germany, Russia, Czechoslovakia, Hungary, and Denmark. The overriding triumph of these American forefathers of the modern Broadway musical is the standard or "hit" song. Audiences tend to remember individual numbers or sections of scores, rather than plots or characters from musicals of the 1920s and 1930s. Often, too, audiences can remember titles of songs, but not the shows they derive from, and so, songs such as "With a Song in My Heart," "My Heart Stood Still," "Thou Swell," "Do, Do, Do," "Someone To Watch Over Me," "The Man I Love," "Swanee," "The Touch of Your Hand," "Smoke Gets In Your Eyes," "Look For The Silver Lining," and "Till the Clouds Roll By," passed into the popular American mainstream without much remembrance of their sources. Between 1924 27, which Gerald Bordman calls "The Golden Age of the American Musical," the outpouring of magnificent melody and brilliant lyrics gave the musical a sophistication and marked the dominance of the AABA pattern and the 32-bar song in popular music. The book — which, by all reasonable accounts, should be a musical's most important element — was often the most forgettable aspect.

Not until Oscar Hammerstein II did the Broadway musical pass to a peak of seriousness. Martin Gottfried calls Hammerstein "The first librettist — perhaps the first *person* — to take the musical theater seriously." Realizing that the book or text of a musical is the basis of a show's existence and provides a context for music, lyric, dance, and dialogue, Hammerstein collaborated with other famous composers to lead the American musical to a level it had never aspired before. His collaboration with Rudolf Friml and Herbert Stothart on *Rose Marie* (1924), and with Sigmund Romberg on *The Desert Song* (1926), owed more to operetta than to literature, but with *Show Boat* in 1927 he connected operetta with drama and literature to give the Broadway musical a new texture, scale, and seriousness. Martin Gottfried is of the opinion that *Show Boat* "opened the door to serious American musical theater" by dealing with serious subjects and tragic elements. It was not a musical comedy, he maintains, "but something new — a *musical play.*" *Show Boat* introduced scenic changes, alternating episode, song, and set change for the duration of the entire show, but it was its book that gave it enduring sturdiness, quite radically striking beyond the obvious appeal of its hit songs such as "Ol' Man River," "Make Believe," or "Can't Help Lovin' Dat Man." As Lerner has said, "It was the only musical of the entire decade whose book was sturdy enough and emotionally true enough to survive the period and remain a permanent musical experience." To which Gottfried adds: "Considering its age, Hammerstein's libretto for *Show Boat* has held up amazingly well. It is certainly superior to the American plays that were being written at the time. Even Eugene O'Neill's works of the same period are more stilted and melodramatic than *Show Boat.*"

In the 1930s *Of Thee I Sing* (1931), by the Gershwins and librettists George S. Kaufman and Mossie Ryskind, combined a sharp libretto with a dazzling score, and went on to astound the world by winning the Pulitzer Prize. Jerome Kern and Hammerstein's *Music in the Air*

(1932) made songs grow organically out of action so that they would not look merely concocted for independent attention, but its operetta-like plot was a limitation. The most significant success was *Porgy and Bess* (1935), from the Gershwins and DuBose Hayward, which was called a "folk opera," though it was more Broadway than opera. The music, which was all of a piece thematically, was carefully composed to support the mood of the text. But apart from these shows and a few others, innovations were sluggish.

Fortunately, Oscar Hammerstein was not done with musical landmarks. In partnership with Richard Rodgers, he produced *Oklahoma!* in 1943, thereby establishing and specializing in musical plays that were, in essence, naturalistic dramas with songs. *Oklahoma!* was, Lerner says, "the most totally realized amalgamation of all the theatrical arts. The book was legitimate play writing, every song flowed from the dramatic action, and Agnes de Mille's ballet at the end of Act One, in which Curly and Laurey were skilfully replaced by two dancers as the plot continued, was one of the most imaginative uses of choreography yet seen in the theatre."

Hammerstein's later works grew increasingly conservative and sentimental in tone, and although many were adaptations of literary works, their scripts cannot now stand on their own as drama. However, their prime emphases were on comedy rather than on drama, and Broadway started once again to drift strongly to trivial entertainments.

To be sure, there were brilliant revues with sketches by Moss Hart, Noel Coward, and Beatrice Lillie. Moreover, Kurt Weill, Bertholt Brecht, and Ira Gershwin busily adapted plays to the musical stage, consolidating the importance of the musical book, but the so-called *belle époch* of the Broadway musical (thriving as it did on shows such as *Finian's Rainbow* [1947], *Brigadoon* [1947], *Kiss Me, Kate* [1948], *South Pacific* [1949], *Guys and Dolls* [1950], *The King and I* [1951], and *Can-Can* [1953]) seems blissfully innocent of high literary patina or subtleties of dramatic construction.

The musicals of the forties had general entertainment uppermost in mind, with fantasy and sentimentality as their overriding qualities. Such shows as *Carousel* (1945), *Annie Get Your Gun* (1946), *Finian's*

Rainbow, and *Brigadoon* had diverse colours, sounds, and styles, but their one unifying element was an escapism from the harsh realities of American society at the time. Popular taste swung between nostalgia — the frontier era of *Annie Get Your Gun*, the 1930s conventionality of *Call Me Madam* (1950), the modish period style for *High Button Shoes* (1947) — and a taste for exotica — the experimentalism of *Beggar's Holiday* (1946), the corniness of *South Pacific*, or the fanciful embroidery on Shakespeare in *Kiss Me, Kate*. Although there were brassy, sassy, coarse, and droll native notes in *Guys and Dolls*, *The Pajama Game* (1954), and *Damn Yankees* (1955), there was an equal interest in settings and sounds that were worlds away from Americana. For example, *The King and I* put its characters in nineteenth-century Siam; *Can-Can* offered comic frippery in a Montmartre café; and *Kismet* (1953) revelled in romantic Oriental hokum.

Several of these shows did nudge the American musical into realms of higher art, but all of them betrayed a conventionality that sharply limited their genius. Many of them cannot be swallowed whole today, primarily because their books were lopsided or flawed, or because their music did not often issue organically from the characters or plot.

It took *My Fair Lady* (1956) to change this.

Appendix II: **CAST AND CREDITS**

My Fair Lady opened in New York on 15 March 1956, at the Mark Hellinger Theatre with the following cast:

(In order of appearance)

Buskers
Imelda de Martin
Carl Jeffrey
Joe Rocco

Mrs. Eynsford-Hill	Viola Roache
Eliza Doolittle	Julie Andrews
Freddy Eynsford-Hill	Michael King
Colonel Pickering	Robert Coote
A Bystander	Leo Britt
Henry Higgins	Rex Harrison
Selsey Man	Gordon Dilworth
Hoxton Man	David Thomas
Another Bystander	Rod McLennan
First Cockney	Reid Shelton
Second Cockney	Glenn Kezer
Third Cockney	James Morris
Fourth Cockney	Herb Surface
Bartender	David Thomas
Harry	Gordon Dilworth
Jamie	Rod McLennan
Alfred P. Doolittle	Stanley Holloway
Mrs. Pearce	Philippa Bevans
Mrs. Hopkins	Olive Reeves-Smith
Butler	Reid Shelton

Servants
Rosemary Gaines
Colleen O'Connor
Muriel Shaw
Gloria van Dorpe
Glenn Kezer

Mrs. Higgins	Cathleen Nesbitt
Chauffeur	Barton Mumaw

Footmen
Gordon Ewing
William Krach

Lord Boxington	Gordon Dilworth
Lady Boxington	Olive Reeves-Smith
Constable	Barton Mumaw
Flower girl	Cathy Conklin
Zoltan Karpathy	Leo Britt
Flunkey	Paul Brown
Queen of Transylvania	Maribel Hammer
Ambassador	Rod McLennan
Bartender	Paul Brown
Mrs. Higgins's Maid	Judith Williams

Singing Ensemble
Melisande Congdon
Lola Fisher
Rosemary Gaines
Maribel Hammer
Colleen O'Connor
Muriel Shaw
Patti Spangler
Gloria van Dorpe
Paul Brown
Gordon Ewing
Glenn Kezer
William Krach
James Morris
Reid Shelton

Herb Surface
David Thomas
Dancing Ensemble
Estelle Aza
Cathy Conklin
Margaret Cuddy
Imelda de Martin
Pat Diamond
Pat Drylie
Barbara Heath
Vera Lee
Nancy Lynch
Judith Williams
Thatcher Clarke
Crandall Diehl
David Evans
Carl Jeffrey
Barton Mumaw
Gene Nettles
Paul Olson
Joe Rocco
Fernando Schaffenburg
James White
PRODUCED BY Herman Levin
DIRECTED BY Moss Hart
SCENERY BY Oliver Smith
COSTUMES BY Cecil Beaton
LIGHTING BY Abe Feder
ORCHESTRA CONDUCTED BY Franz Allers
ORCHESTRATIONS BY Robert Russell Bennet and Phil Lang

WORKS CONSULTED

Atkinson, Brooks. "Everybody's 'Lady.'" *New York Times* 3 June 1956.

——. "My Fair Lady." *New York Times* 16 Mar. 1956.

Beaton, Cecil. *Cecil Beaton's 'Fair Lady.'* London: Weidenfeld, 1964.

——. *The Glass of Fashion*. London: Cassell, 1989.

——. *The Restless Years: Diaries 1955 63*. London: Weidenfeld, 1976.

Beaufort, John. "'My Fair Lady' from 'Pygmalion.'" *Christian Science Monitor* 24 Mar. 1956.

Beckerman, Bernard, and Howard Siegman, eds. *On Stage: Selected Theatre Reviews from the New York Times 1920 1970*. New York: Arno, 1983.

Bentley, Eric. *Bernard Shaw*. New York: New Directions, 1957.

——. "My Fair Lady." *Modern Drama* 1.2 (1958): 135 36.

——. *What Is Theatre?* New York: Limelight, 1984.

Bordman, Gerald. *American Musical Theatre*. New York: Oxford UP, 1978.

Brahms, Caryl. "Fair-Lady-Mindedness." *Plays and Players* 5.9 (1958): 7.

Buckle, Richard, ed. *Self-Portrait with Friends: Selected Diaries of Cecil Beaton 1926 1974*. Harmondsworth: Penguin, 1982.

Castle, Charles. *Noel*. London: W.H. Allen, 1972.

Chapman, John. "'My Fair Lady' a Superb, Stylish Musical Play with a Perfect Cast." *Daily News* [New York] 16 Mar. 1956.

Chesterton, G.K. *George Bernard Shaw*. New York: Hill and Wang, 1958.

Coleman, Robert. "'My Fair Lady' Is a Glittering Musical." *Daily Mirror* 16 Mar. 1956.

Dash, Thomas R. Rev. of *My Fair Lady*. *Women's Wear Daily* 16 Mar. 1956.

Engel, Lehman. *Words with Music*. New York: Macmillan, 1972.

Ewen, David. *Complete Book of the American Musical Theatre*. Rev. ed. New York: Holt, 1959.

Gänzl, Kurt. *The Blackwell Guide to the Musical Theatre on Record*. Oxford: Blackwell, 1990.

Gibbs, Wolcott. "Shaw with Music." *New Yorker* 24 Mar. 1956.

Gottfried, Martin. *Broadway Musicals*. New York: Abrams, 1979.

Green, Benny, ed. *A Hymn to Him: The Lyrics of Alan Jay Lerner*. London: Pavilion, 1987.

Green, Stanley. *Encyclopedia of the Musical Theatre*. New York: Da Capo, 1976.

———. *The World of Musical Comedy*. 3rd rev. ed. New York: Barnes, 1974.

Guernsey, Otis L., Jr. *Curtain Times: The New York Theatre 1965 1987*. New York: Applause, 1987.

Hadleigh, Boze. *Conversations with My Elders*. New York: St. Martin's, 1986.

Harrison, Rex. *A Damned Serious Business*. New York: Bantam, 1991.

———. *Rex: An Autobiography*. London: Macmillan, 1974.

Hart, Kitty Carlisle. *Kitty: An Autobiography*. New York: Doubleday, 1988.

Hart, Moss. *Act One: An Autobiography*. New York: Random, 1959.

Hawkins, William. "'My Fair Lady' Is a Smash Hit." *New York World Telegram and The Sun* 16 Mar. 1956.

Holloway, Stanley. *Wiv a Little Bit O' Luck*. London: Leslie Frewin, 1967.

Holroyd, Michael. *The Genius of Shaw*. London: Hodder, 1979.

———. *The Pursuit of Power: 1898 1918*. Vol. 2 of *Bernard Shaw*. London: Chatto, 1989.

———. *The Lure of Fantasy: 1918 1950*. Vol. 3 of *Bernard Shaw*. London: Chatto, 1991.

Irvine, William. *The Universe of G.B.S.* New York: Whittlesey, 1949.

Jackson, Arthur. *The Best Musicals: From 'Show Boat' to 'A Chorus Line.'* New York: Crown, 1977.

Kaufman, R.J., ed. *G.B. Shaw: A Collection of Critical Essays*. Englewood Cliffs, NJ: Prentice, 1965.

Kerr, Walter. *Journey to the Center of the Theatre*. New York: Knopf, 1979.

———. "My Fair Lady." *Herald Tribune* [New York] 16 Mar. 1956.

Kronenberger, Louis. *The Thread of Laughter: Chapters on English Stage Comedy from Jonson to Maugham*. New York: Knopf, 1952.

Laufe, Abe. *Broadway's Greatest Musicals*. Illus. New York: Funk, 1970.

Leary, Daniel, ed. *Shaw's Plays in Performance*. Vol. 3 of *Annual of Bernard Shaw Studies*. University Park: Pennsylvania State UP, 1983.

Lees, Gene. *Inventing Champagne: The Worlds of Lerner and Loewe*. New York: St. Martin's, 1990.

Lerner, Alan Jay. *The Musical Theatre: A Celebration*. New York: McGraw, 1986.

———. *My Fair Lady: A Musical Play in Two Acts*. New York: Signet, 1958.

———. "Programme Note." *Playbill* 1.6 (1957): 17.

———. *The Street Where I Live*. London: Hodder, 1978.

McCarthy, Desmond. *Shaw*. London: MacGibbon & Kee, 1951.

McClain, John. "It's Fetching — Well Done!" *New York Journal-American* 16 Mar. 1956.

Meisel, Martin. *Shaw and the Nineteenth Century Theatre*. New York: Limelight, 1984.

"Moon over Wimpole Street." Rev. of *My Fair Lady*. *Saturday Review* 7 Apr. 1956.

Mordden, Ethan. *Broadway Babies: The People Who Made the American Musical*. New York: Oxford UP, 1983.

Morgan, Margery M. *The Shavian Playground: An Exploration of the Art of George Bernard Shaw*. London: Methuen, 1972.

Morley, Sheridan. *A Talent to Amuse: A Biography of Noel Coward*. Harmondsworth: Penguin, 1975.

Nathan, George Jean. Column in *New York Journal-American* 5 May 1956.

———. "The Season's Top Show." *New York Journal-American* 31 Mar. 1956.

Pascal, Valerie. *The Disciple and His Devil*. New York: McGraw, 1970.

Pearson, Hesketh. *Bernard Shaw: His Life and Personality*. London: Collins, 1942.

Rev. of *My Fair Lady*, by F.S. *Theatre World* 54.401 (1958): 23.

Rev. of *My Fair Lady*. *Variety* 21 Mar. 1956.

Shaw, Bernard. *Pygmalion*. Harmondsworth: Penguin, 1963.

Smith, Oliver. "The Designer Talks." Interview by Robert Waterhouse. *Plays and Players* 18.2 (1970): 20 21.

Sorrell, Walter. *Hanya Holm: The Biography of an Artist*. Middletown, CT. Wesleyan UP, 1969.

Stephens, Frances, ed. *Theatre World Annual*. Vol. 9. London: Rockcliff, 1958.

Suskin, Steven. *Opening Night on Broadway*. New York: Schirmer, 1990.

Swain, Joseph P. *The Broadway Musical: A Critical and Musical Survey*. New York: Oxford UP, 1990.

Tynan, Kenneth. *Tynan Right & Left*. London: Longmans, 1967.

———. *A View of the English Stage*. Frogmore, St. Albans: Paladin, 1976.

Valency, Maurice. *The Cart and the Trumpet: The Plays of George Bernard Shaw*. New York: Schocken, 1983.

Vickers, Hugo. *Cecil Beaton: The Authorized Biography*. London: Weidenfeld, 1985.

Watts, Richard, Jr. "When Everything Goes Just Right." *New York Post* 16 Mar. 1956.

Weintraub, Stanley. *Shaw: An Autobiography 1856 1898*. Vol. 1. New York: Weybright and Talley, 1969.

——— . *The Playwright Years 1898 1950*. Vol. 2 of *Shaw: An Autobiography*. New York: Weybright and Talley, 1970.

Windeler, Robert. *Julie Andrews: A Biography*. New York: St. Martin's, 1983.

Zadan, Craig. *Sondheim & Co.* 2nd ed. New York: Harper, 1989.

Printed in Canada